Albert Einstein

with profiles of
Isaac Newton
and J. Robert Oppenheimer

World Book, Inc.
a Scott Fetzer company
Chicago

BIOGRAPHICAL ⊕ CONNECTIONS

Writer: Naomi Pasachoff.

© 2007 World Book, Inc. All rights reserved. The content of this publication may not be reproduced in whole or in part in any form without prior written permission from the publisher. WORLD BOOK and the GLOBE DEVICE are registered trademarks or trademarks of World Book, Inc.

World Book, Inc.
233 N. Michigan Ave.
Chicago, IL 60601

For information about other World Book publications, visit our Web site at **www.worldbook.com** or call **1-800-WORLDBK (967-5325)**.
For information about sales to schools and libraries, call **1-800-975-3250 (United States)**, or **1-800-837-5365 (Canada)**.

Library of Congress Cataloging-in-Publication Data

Pasachoff, Naomi E.
   Albert Einstein: with profiles of Isaac Newton and J. Robert Oppenheimer/ [writer, Naomi Pasachoff].
      p. cm. -- (Biographical connections)
   Includes bibliographical references and index.
   Summary: "A biography of Albert Einstein, with profiles of two prominent individuals, who are associated through the influences they had on one another, the successes they achieved, or the goals they worked toward. Includes recommended readings and web sites"--Provided by publisher.
   ISBN-13: 978-0-7166-1825-6
   ISBN-10: 0-7166-1825-7
   1. Einstein, Albert, 1879-1955. 2. Oppenheimer, J. Robert, 1904-1967.
3. Newton, Isaac, Sir, 1642-1727--Influence. 4. Physicists--Biography.
I. World Book, Inc. II. Title. III. Series.
QC16.E5P374 2007
530.092'2--dc22
[B]
                                                    2006015548
Printed in the United States of America
1 2 3 4 5 10 09 08 07 06

Contents

Acknowledgments

The publisher gratefully acknowledges the following sources for the photographs in this volume.

Cover	© Corbis
	© Mary Evans Picture Library
	© Corbis/Bettmann
7	© Mary Evans Picture Library
8	© National Trust Photographic Library/The Image Works
11	Granger Collection
15	© Corbis/Bettmann
22	© Jim Sugar, Corbis
25	© Yousuh Karsh, Camera Press/Retna Ltd.
26	© Alfred Eisenstaedt, Getty Images
28	© Alfred Einstein Archives/Jewish National University
31	© ETH-Bibliothek
34	© Alfred Einstein Archives/Jewish National University
38	© ETH-Bibliothek
43	© Corbis/Underwood & Underwood
48	© Corbis/Hulton-Deutsch Collection
52	© Hulton Archive/Getty Images
56-59	© Corbis/Bettmann
65	© Time Life Picture Library/Getty Images
66	© Paul Ehrenfest, AIP Emilio Segre Visual Archives
71-78	© Corbis/Bettmann
82	© MPI/Getty Images
84	© Corbis/Bettmann
86	© Time Life Picture Picture Library/Getty Images
89	© Corbis/Bettmann
90	© Corbis
95	© Alfred Eisenstaedt, Getty Images
101-102	© Corbis/Bettmann
103	© Time Life Picture Library/Getty Images
105	© Corbis/Bettmann

Preface

Biographical Connections takes a contextual approach in presenting the lives of important people. In each volume, there is a biography of a central figure. This biography is preceded and followed by profiles of other individuals whose lifework connects in some way to that of the central figure. The three subjects are associated through the influences they had on one another, the successes they achieved, or the goals they worked toward. The series includes men and women from around the world and throughout history in a variety of fields.

This volume features three scientists, centered around the work of German-born physicist Albert Einstein, who created revolutionary theories of physics during the early 1900's that transformed our understanding of nature and led to countless technological breakthroughs. Einstein's theories expanded on the classical foundation of physics laid in the late 1600's by the English scientist Isaac Newton, whose profile precedes Einstein's biography in this volume. The American physicist J. Robert Oppenheimer built upon Einstein's work in the realms of both scientific theory and technology. During the 1930's and 1940's, Oppenheimer used concepts from Einstein's theories of relativity to predict the existence of *black holes* and to lead a project that developed the first atomic bomb. Black holes are invisible regions of space in which the gravitational force is so strong that not even light can escape from them. Oppenheimer's profile follows Einstein's biography in this volume.

All three of these scientists based their discoveries on the physical laws of motion and gravity. Classical mechanics is based to a large extent on the physical laws described by Isaac Newton. Newton's laws remained unchallenged for more than 200 years.

In June 1905, Einstein revolutionized the world of physics with his special theory of relativity. This theory challenged Newton's laws by proposing that space, time, and motion are relative—that is, they change—instead of absolute. In place of Newton's concepts of absolute space and time, Einstein proposed the concept of space-time, which links space and time in an inseparable way.

In the late 1800's and early 1900's, scientists working in the new field of radioactivity figured out that the *nucleus* of a uranium atom could be split into nuclei of lighter atoms. According to Einstein's equation $E = mc^2$, this splitting is accompanied by the tremendous release of energy. This process, called *nuclear fission*, could be harnessed to produce a weapon of mass destruction, the atomic bomb, as well as energy for peaceful purposes.

In 1939, at the beginning of World War II (1939–1945), Einstein wrote a letter to President Franklin D. Roosevelt expressing his fear that German scientists might be developing an atomic bomb. Einstein's letter was one factor that led the United States to establish the Manhattan Project in 1942, after the United States entered World War II. The Manhattan Project was a secret program organized by the U.S. War Department to produce an atomic bomb.

In autumn 1942, the director of the Manhattan Project offered J. Robert Oppenheimer the directorship of the bomb design unit. Oppenheimer accepted the position and went on to assemble a large team of talented scientists in Los Alamos, New Mexico. There, under his skillful management, they succeeded in the task. Two atomic bombs were dropped on Japan in 1945, killing between 120,000 and 140,000 people. Following the war, Einstein and Oppenheimer both spoke out against the use of nuclear weapons.

Oppenheimer's connection to Einstein is also related to another of Einstein's revolutionary ideas. In 1915, Einstein expanded on his special theory of relativity to resolve a conflict between his theory and Newton's law of gravitation. J. Robert Oppenheimer used Einstein's general theory of relativity to make a remarkable prediction of his own. In a 1939 paper, "On Continued Gravitational Contraction," Oppenheimer and a student collaborator used Einstein's theory of general relativity to predict the existence of black holes.

These three scientists—Newton, Einstein, and Oppenheimer—built upon the ideas of their forerunners to create theories that transformed our understanding of the universe. The work of each physicist also contributed to technological developments that altered the course of history and continue to impact our daily lives. ■

Isaac Newton (1642–1727)

The English physicist and mathematician Isaac Newton was one of the greatest scientists of all time. He used his laws of motion and his law of gravitation to describe everything from the orbit of planets around the sun to, according to legend, the falling of an apple from a tree. He also invented *calculus,* the system of mathematics used by scientists to solve many problems, and the first working reflecting telescope.

Newton's theories provided strong evidence that the universe is orderly and knowable by science and mathematics. They also formed the rock upon which classical physics was built.

By the late 1800's, however, Newton's laws proved inadequate to explain some of the phenomena, such as *electromagnetic* waves, that scientists had discovered. It would take another great scientist, Albert Einstein, to expand Newton's explanations into the modern world.

EARLY LIFE

Isaac Newton was born on Dec. 25, 1642, in Woolsthorpe, England. His mother, Hannah Ayscough, named her infant son after his father, who had died nearly three months earlier. Newton's father had not been an educated man, but he came from a fairly well-off family. The Newtons had owned property at Woolsthorpe, in Lincolnshire, a county in eastern England, for several generations. The older Isaac Newton's marriage into the Ayscough family brought not only additional wealth to the Newton family but also the family's first contact with education. Hannah's brother, William, a graduate of the centuries-old University of Cambridge, was a member of the Anglican clergy.

According to a story about himself that Newton told when he was in his 80's, "when he was born he was so little they could put

The house in which Isaac Newton was born on Christmas Day 1642 is in the town of Woolsthorpe in eastern England.

him into a quart pot & so weakly that he was forced to have a bolster all round his neck to keep it on his shoulders."[1] This child, who was not expected to live, would grow up to have quite a head on his shoulders.

When Isaac was 3, his mother married Barnabas Smith, a well-off widower who lived in a nearby village. Like Hannah's brother, Smith was a clergyman. Educated at the University of Oxford, Smith had a large library, which his stepson Isaac would eventually inherit. In a mostly blank notebook in which Smith had made a few entries of his own, Newton would make his first steps toward discovering the basic theorem of *calculus* and formulating his laws of motion and gravitation. (Calculus, the branch of mathematics that deals with changing quantities, is the language in which scientists develop theories and solve practical problems.)

In the nearly eight years of their marriage, which ended with Smith's death in 1653, the couple had three children. But Smith was not interested in raising Isaac in the residence where he and Hannah made their home. Hannah, therefore, left her toddler in the Newton manor house in Woolsthorpe with her parents.

Hannah rejoined her 10-year-old first-born in Woolsthorpe after her husband's death in 1653. Less than two years later, Isaac was sent off to grammar school in nearby Grantham. He boarded with the local *apothecary* (pharmacist) and his family. In school at Grantham, Isaac studied mostly Latin and the Bible. His expertise in Latin later would allow him to communicate with other European scientists who did not know English. His biblical training inspired the theological studies that would take up much of his time.

Years later, people who had known young Isaac Newton in Grantham remembered the wooden models he made. He copied the windmill north of town and equipped his model with a treadmill operated by a mouse. Newton also made a four-wheeled cart that he moved with a crank. He fashioned a lantern of "crimpled paper," which could illuminate his path to school on dark winter mornings or frighten the neighbors when attached to a kite tail. He became known for making sundials, and townspeople eventually consulted "Isaac's dials" to identify the days of the month. In Grantham, Isaac also had the only romantic relationship with a female that he ever would have. He made no friends among the boys, however.

In late 1659, just before Newton's 17th birthday, his mother summoned him back to Woolsthorpe. She expected him to manage the estate. During nine months at home, Isaac showed no inclination to herd sheep or shovel dung. Luckily, Hannah's brother, the Reverend Ayscough, intervened. So did the Grantham schoolmaster, Mr. Stokes. Both thought Isaac was university material. On their advice, Hannah sent Isaac back to Grantham. This time Isaac boarded with Mr. Stokes, who charged Hannah no fees for Isaac's tuition or board. After his additional time at Grantham, Isaac left for the University of Cambridge in June 1661.

TRINITY COLLEGE UNDERGRADUATE

On June 5, 1661, Newton was admitted to Trinity College, Cambridge. Another Cambridge student at the time called Trinity "the famousest College in the University."[2] Newton's uncle, the Reverend William Ayscough, had also been a Trinity man. Newton began his university career as a *subsizar*—a poor student who supported himself by doing chores for other members of the college. Newton was used to having servants tend to his needs at Woolsthorpe. Now he had to tend to the needs of others. His well-to-do mother must have denied him an allowance. She had not wanted him to go to university. As a result of her stinginess, Newton found himself at the bottom of the college social ladder. He probably was a lonely student at Cambridge.

Over 235 years later, Albert Einstein would find the prescribed courses at the Swiss Federal Polytechnic Institute a waste of his time and concentrated instead on books of his own choosing. Newton's university experience was similar. He did not finish any of the books on the established curriculum. Instead, he became very familiar with the work of the recently deceased French philosopher, mathematician, and scientist René Descartes. Descartes believed that the physical universe could be understood through concepts he borrowed from geometry, along with his own laws of motion.

Newton's extracurricular reading also exposed him to the *Dialogue Concerning the Two Chief World Systems,* a 1632 masterpiece by Italian astronomer and physicist Galileo Galilei. This work argued that the Copernican theory, which placed the sun in the center of the universe, was logically superior to the Ptolemaic-Aristotelian theory, which had Earth at the center.

Newton began a notebook in which he collected notes and questions inspired by his own reading. According to the late Richard Westfall, a major Newton scholar, the thoughts Newton collected in this notebook "foreshadowed the problems on which his career in science would focus and the method by which he would attack them."[3]

Newton also began reading books about geometry, including Descartes's recent invention, analytic geometry. In 1663, Cambridge established a new chair—a professorial position—in mathematics. It was called the Lucasian Chair of Mathematics, and Newton would before long become the second professor to hold that chair. In March 1664, the first Lucasian professor, Isaac Barrow, gave the first in a series of lectures on mathematics. Newton probably attended them.

In April 1664, Newton was elected to a scholarship at Trinity. He was no longer a subsizar—the college supported him for several more years of study. He earned his B.A. degree in 1665. That summer, however, the university was forced to shut down because of an outbreak of plague. Newton returned to Woolsthorpe, where he remained through spring 1667. While there, Newton conducted revolutionary work in mathematics, physics, and optics.

WONDROUS DISCOVERIES OF THE PLAGUE YEARS

Historians have referred to this period in Woolsthorpe as Newton's "year of miracles" (or, in Latin, *annus mirabilis*). Looking back on those years decades later, Newton wrote a French colleague, "For in those days I was in the prime of my age of invention and minded mathematics and philosophy more than at any time since."[4]

During this period, Newton formulated the fundamental theorem of calculus: the statement that the two central operations of calculus, *differentiation* and *integration,* are inverses. He did preparatory work on this problem in Cambridge, just before the university was shut down. Before he turned 24 in 1666, Newton surpassed the achievements of Descartes and became the world's most advanced mathematician. This fact was unknown, however, since Newton did not attempt to publish his results.

Shortly before his death, Newton told a friend that "the notion of gravitation came into his mind" at Woolsthorpe during the plague years. "It was occasioned by the fall of an apple, as he sat in a contemplative mood."[5] Newton developed his concept of gravity by imagining the moon as a giant apple. He realized that the force that pulls an apple to Earth is the same as the force that keeps the moon in orbit. Realizing that the same force governs the planets as they circle the sun, he understood that gravitation was a universal principle.

Newton discovered that the force of universal gravitation depends both on the amount of matter in the bodies being attracted and the distance between those bodies. He calculated that the force of gravity is proportional to the inverse-square of the distance (that is, 1 over the distance squared) between two bodies. For example, two objects that are moved twice as far apart will feel one-fourth the force of gravity they felt at their original positions. Newton later described this discovery of the plague years: "I deduced the forces which keep the planets in their orbs must be reciprocally as the squares of their distances from the centers about which they revolve."[6] Newton was dissatisfied with the way his gravitational calculations were working out, however. Over 20 years would pass before he published his discoveries about gravity and motion.

Newton used a glass prism to bend rays of sunlight, revealing that the white light is actually made up of a spectrum of different colors.

On a visit to a fair before the epidemic forced it to close, Newton bought "a triangular glass prism to try therewith the celebrated phenomena of colors."[7] Aristotle, a Greek philosopher of the mid-300's B.C., suggested that color is related to light, but no one yet understood the true nature of color. Newton used his prism to investigate the nature of light. He darkened his south-facing bedroom, drilled a hole in a shutter, and intercepted the incoming sunlight with the prism. His experiments proved that white light consists of all the colors of the *spectrum*. He figured out that each of the seven colors of the spectrum was bent at a different angle on passing through the prism. He then accurately calculated the angles of the bent colored rays and formulated a new law of *refraction*.

Newton's work with color, like his work on gravitation and motion, supported his growing conviction that nature operates according to firm mathematical principles. But just as he did not publicize his discoveries about calculus, gravity, and motion, he did not publish his discoveries about color during the plague years.

PROFESSOR AND PROFESSIONAL SCIENTIST

After the threat of plague had passed, Newton returned to the newly reopened Trinity College. In fall 1667, he was made a Fellow of the college, a staff position that allowed him to remain permanently in the academic community. In July 1668, Newton was awarded his M.A. degree.

Unlike other Fellows of Trinity College, Newton was not ordained into the ministry of the Church of England. His theological studies had led him to reject the doctrine of the Trinity—that there is one Divine Being with a threefold personality (Father, Son, Holy Ghost). That doctrine is a major principle of Christianity. Without explaining his reason for doing so, Newton petitioned the king to waive the requirement that he take holy orders. The request was granted. Had his true reason for resisting ordination been discovered, Newton's career would have ended before it began.

Isaac Barrow, the first Lucasian Professor of Mathematics, had taken an interest in Newton's work. In 1669, Barrow left Cambridge for London, to take up a prestigious appointment as chaplain to

King Charles II. Newton, then only 27 years old, succeeded Barrow as Lucasian Professor.

In early 1670, the new Lucasian Professor chose optics as the subject for his series of eight inaugural lectures. During the three years since his initial experiments with prisms at Woolsthorpe, Newton continued his investigations into the nature of light and color. He was satisfied that the additional research put him in a position "to bring forth my opinion more distinctly."[8] Since hardly anyone showed up to hear the lectures, Newton remained basically unknown. However, the Royal Society would soon learn of him.

In 1662, King Charles II granted a charter to the Royal Society of London for the Promotion of Natural Knowledge. Three years later, the society began to publish one of the earliest scientific periodicals, *Philosophical Transactions,* which became the model for other scientific journals. Society members included the most distinguished scientific minds of the day, including architect and astronomer Christopher Wren and inventor and physicist Robert Hooke.

What brought Newton's name before the membership of the Royal Society was news that he had constructed the first working reflecting telescope. Newton had undertaken this challenge because of a drawback of refracting telescopes, which had first been used for astronomy by Galileo in 1609. Refractors, which form images of objects using lenses, suffer from *chromatic aberration*—that is, different colors are imaged at different points. Reflectors, however, use mirrors, which are not affected by chromatic aberration. Newton, using skills he had perfected in boyhood, succeeded in preparing a reflector. In an early 1669 letter to a friend, he reported having "seen with it Jupiter distinctly round and his satellites."[9]

At the urging of the society, in 1671 Newton entrusted Isaac Barrow with a second, somewhat modified, reflector that he made. Barrow presented it to the society, which demonstrated the telescope's capabilities to the king. The reclusive Newton not only accepted membership in the Royal Society but also sent a paper describing his optical discoveries and agreed to its publication in the *Philosophical Transactions.* This decision launched Newton on what was to become the first of several bitter professional controversies.

Robert Hooke, as curator of experiments for the Royal Society, was responsible for confirming Newton's experiments with prisms. Although he agreed with Newton's experimental results, Hooke challenged one of Newton's key assertions—that light is composed of minute particles. According to Hooke, "even those very experiments which he alleged do seem to me to prove that light is nothing but a pulse or motion propagated through a . . . uniform and transparent medium."[10] Newton's response, published in the *Philosophical Transactions*, left Hooke feeling humiliated. In addition, Hooke claimed that he had constructed a smaller and more accurate reflector. Newton and Hooke remained lifelong enemies.

When the secretary of the Royal Society sent Newton critical comments from other scientists, Newton was so unsettled that he threatened to resign from the society. The secretary cancelled Newton's dues and resolved not to forward any more objections to his paper on light. Nonetheless, Newton withdrew into seclusion, corresponding with scarcely anyone. Two years passed before Newton submitted two new papers about light to the society. The second paper made use of Hooke's 1665 treatise on light, *Micrographia,* but failed to acknowledge his debt to the scientist. Hooke wrote directly to Newton, and the two men agreed to no longer carry out their feud in print. The truce was to prove short-lived.

THE *PRINCIPIA MATHEMATICA*

In summer 1684, the English astronomer Edmond Halley visited Newton in Cambridge. Earlier that year, Halley had shared two convictions with two other Fellows of the Royal Society, Robert Hooke and Sir Christopher Wren: (1) the inverse-square law plays an important role in celestial mechanics, and (2) therefore, the planets must orbit the sun in elliptical orbits. Having learned that both older men had come to the same conclusions, Halley now sought out the Lucasian Professor, in hopes that Newton could provide mathematical proof for these shared convictions.

Halley was amazed when Newton told him that he had already worked out the calculations that proved that the planets' orbits took the shape of an elliptical curve. Unable to find his original calculations, however, Newton promised to rework them and forward them to Halley in London. Over the next three months Newton solved the problem using a different mathematical method than he had before. He also wrote a manuscript, "On the Motion of Revolving Bodies," which arrived in London that November. Halley immediately returned to Cambridge to secure Newton's permission to publish the paper in *Philosophical Transactions*.

Newton decided to withhold the paper for the moment. In 1685, he wrote to John Flamsteed, England's first *astronomer royal* (the chief astronomer of England), "Now that I am upon this subject, I would gladly know the bottom of it before I publish my papers."[11] For the next 18 months, he worked diligently—ignoring food, sleep, and personal grooming. The result was the first third of what would turn out to be the most significant scientific work yet written. Its Latin title, *Philosophiae Naturalis Principia Mathematica*—meaning *Mathematical Principles of Natural Philosophy*—is usually shortened to "the *Principia*." The *Principia* was the first book to contain a comprehensive system of scientific principles to explain many of the physical phenomena observed on Earth and in the heavens.

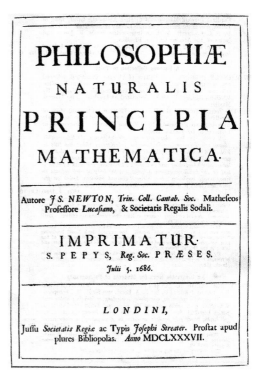

Newton's Philosophiae Naturalis Principia Mathematica, *or the* Principia, *first appeared in print in 1687, offering readers scientific explanations for understanding Earth and the stars.*

At first, the Royal Society agreed to pay for the book's publication. Then, when the Fellows learned that the society lacked the funds to do so, Halley agreed to personally finance the project. He also undertook the daunting task of editing the manuscript of a scientist known for his prickly temper.

Hooke greeted the first installment of the *Principia* with the claim that Newton had plagiarized him. According to Hooke, not only had he discovered the inverse-square law six years before, but he had also sent his calculations to Newton. Hooke's claim led Newton to threaten to withhold the rest of the book. Halley attempted to defuse the situation, urging Newton to act graciously by acknowledging

Hooke in the preface. Newton's response was to delete every reference to Hooke in the *Principia*. Having done so, he allowed publication to proceed. The book was finally published in July 1687. It included an "Ode to Newton" by Halley. The poem concluded, "Nearer to the gods no mortal may approach."[12]

The *Principia* contains Newton's famous three laws of motion. The first, called the *principle of inertia,* states that an object moving at a constant speed and in the same direction will continue to do so unless acted upon by an outside force. It also states that an object at rest will remain at rest unless moved by a force. The second law describes how an object changes its motion when a force is applied to it. Scientists use the formula that expresses the second law, $F = ma,$ to describe the motion of many kinds of objects. F stands for the applied force, m for the mass, and a for the resulting acceleration. The third law states that for each action there is an equal and opposite reaction. For example, if one object exerts a force on a second object, the second object must exert an equal and opposite force on the first object.

In the first pages of the *Principia,* Newton explained two terms: *time* and *space,* which form the basis of his laws of motion. According to Newton, "Absolute, true, and mathematical time, of itself and from its own nature, flows equably, without relation to anything external, and by another name is called duration." He described two different kinds of space: "absolute space, in its own nature, without relation to anything external," which "remains always similar and immovable," and "relative space," which was "some movable dimension or measure of the absolute spaces."[13]

More than 200 years later, Einstein's 1905 special theory of relativity substituted the concept of space-time for the concepts of absolute time and absolute space. Einstein suggested several modifications to Newton's laws of motion, particularly the second law. For example, Einstein showed that an object's mass appears to increase as its velocity increases, something subsequently verified for objects traveling at velocities near the speed of light. But Einstein never claimed that his work replaced Newton's. Rather, he said his results merely expanded upon the predictions of Newtonian physics.

Newton's laws of motion still hold for slow-moving objects. However, there are deep conceptual differences between the two approaches in their definitions of such terms as *space, time,* and *mass.*

The laws detailed in Newton's *Principia* provided proof that the universe is both orderly and, through mathematics, knowable. Halley immediately deduced one consequence of Newton's theories: the laws that apply to planets must also apply to comets. In the late 1600's, Halley collected data on a large number of previously observed comets. Using Newton's laws, he calculated their orbits. His research enabled him to confirm Newton's view of the universe by identifying a comet that appeared regularly, at intervals of about 76 years. Halley predicted that this comet would return in 1758 and every 76 years thereafter. The comet was sighted on Christmas day 1758, which was also the 116th anniversary of Newton's birth. The comet became known as Halley's *(HAL eez)* Comet.

TRANSITION TO PUBLIC LIFE

Not long after the publication of the *Principia*, Newton's life took a turn, following a dramatic moment in the history of England. In the Glorious Revolution of 1688, King James II was forced to give up the throne. His daughter Mary and her husband, William of Orange, ruler of the Netherlands, became joint rulers in 1689. On Jan. 15, 1689, the Cambridge University senate selected Newton as one of two university delegates to a special session of Parliament, England's lawmaking body. It was to be one of the most important sessions of Parliament in British history.

Later known as the Convention Parliament of 1689, the session's goal was to resolve the political crisis. The Parliament not only declared William and Mary the new monarchs, but also proclaimed the limited nature of the British monarchy—a monarchy whose powers were limited by law. In addition, Parliament abolished the standing army in peacetime and enacted a Bill of Rights (which would later become a model for the first 10 amendments to the Constitution of the United States).

Despite the momentous nature of the occasion, Newton's spoken participation was limited to a single comment: he asked an usher to close the window. But during that year in London, Newton made friends in high places and attempted to secure a new position. Several years would pass before he succeeded in doing so.

In September 1693, following an intense but ultimately fruitless period of research that spring and summer, Newton wrote former Royal Society President Samuel Pepys: "I . . . have neither ate nor slept well this twelve month, nor have my former consistency of mind."[14] In fact, Newton was suffering from a severe mental and physical breakdown. He wrote disturbing letters, filled with baseless accusations, to some of his friends.

Along with his scientific activities, Newton secretly engaged in *alchemy*. Alchemy was a blend of chemistry and pseudoscience popular from the A.D. 300's until about 1700. Alchemists were especially interested in discovering methods for transforming baser metals into gold and for prolonging life. The more serious alchemists, including Newton, were forerunners of modern-day chemists. When his alchemical work went badly in 1693, Newton put it away forever. In all likelihood, the failure of his experiments after such concentrated effort left Newton feeling depressed and depleted. He now wished to put his life in Cambridge behind him as soon as possible.

Thanks to Charles Montague, a powerful friend and intimate of the king, that opportunity arose in 1696. Newton was appointed to the second highest position in the royal mint. He permanently left Cambridge, his home for the previous 35 years. Newton packed up his manuscripts—including many hundreds of pages on alchemy— but left behind his furniture and alchemical equipment.

Newton's new place of employment was situated within the Tower of London, which is today a popular tourist site. The secret alchemist had to swear to a different type of secrecy: Like all employees of the mint, Newton took an oath not to reveal how new coins were made. Counterfeiting was a serious problem in England at the time. Newton acquainted himself with London's criminal underworld and succeeded in obtaining the arrest and execution of William Chaloner, a master counterfeiter.

Newton's position at the mint required him to do a fair amount of official entertaining. As a bachelor, Newton needed someone to tend to his household and entertain his guests. His niece Catherine Barton filled the bill. (Catherine was the daughter of his half-sister, Hannah Smith.) A beautiful and intelligent woman, Catherine was admired by many of Newton's guests. After her marriage in 1717, she divided her time between Newton's home and the ancestral home of her husband, John Conduitt.

On Christmas Day, 1699, 57-year-old Newton was elevated to the highest position at the mint when its previous master died. In 1701, the University of Cambridge once again elected Newton to Parliament. At the end of that year, Newton finally gave up his Lucasian Professorship at Cambridge. He had not wanted to do so until he was certain that his government position was secure.

Newton brought the long academic chapter and the shorter political chapter of his life to a close at the same time. When the Cambridge authorities asked if he had any interest in serving in Parliament again, Newton declined: "And now I have served you in this Parliament, other gentlemen may expect their turn in the next."[15] He returned to Trinity College in 1705, however. On that occasion, he was knighted by Queen Anne. From that time on, he was known as Sir Isaac Newton.

PRESIDENT OF THE ROYAL SOCIETY

Ever since he began work at the mint, Newton had steered clear of the Royal Society. His excuse was that his position was too demanding. In fact, Newton shunned the society in order to avoid contact with his old enemy, Robert Hooke. After Hooke's death in 1703 at the age of 68, the Fellows of the Royal Society elected Newton president.

The society he took over was in poor shape. The treasury was bare. Few members attended its meetings. The topics of discussion were far removed from the latest developments in science. Newton began a series of reforms by issuing a "Scheme for establishing the Royal Society." The first order of business was to revive the society's mission of "discovering the frame & operations of Nature, reducing them (as far as may be) to general Rules or Laws, establishing those Rules by observations & experiments, and then deducing the causes

& effects of things."[16] To facilitate this scheme, he recommended that four "demonstrators" be hired to present experiments and lectures in a variety of scientific disciplines.

Newton restored the society to financial health. New members were required to pay an admission fee before induction. All members were required to sign a bond that committed them to pay weekly dues. No one whose dues were not paid could serve on the society's council. Foreign membership rose dramatically during Newton's administration. He welcomed not only scientists but also political figures into the organization. Under Newton's presidency, the society also found its first permanent headquarters. With assistance from Sir Christopher Wren, Newton arranged for the purchase of the property.

According to one Fellow: "Whilst [Newton] presided in the Royal Society, he executed that office with singular prudence, with grace and dignity. . . . Sir Isaac was very careful of giving any sort of discouragement to all attempts of improvement in natural knowledg[e]. There was no whispering, talking, nor loud laughters. Every thing was transacted with great attention and solemnity and decency. . . . Indeed his presence created a natural awe in the assembly. . . ."[17]

In 1704, Newton presented the Royal Society with his second major work on physical science, the *Opticks*. This time he personally prepared the manuscript for publication. As Newton indicated in the preface, the book was based primarily on work he did as a young man. He had published some of his discoveries in 1672. Why had he postponed publication of the volume for over 30 years? The answer lies in the preface: "To avoid being engaged in Disputes about these Matters, I have hitherto delayed the Printing, and should still have delayed it, had not the importunity of Friends prevailed upon me."[18] He was still rankled by the memory of Hooke's criticism of his theory of light.

Even if Newton had not published the *Principia*, he would have earned his reputation as one of the greatest scientists of all time for the *Opticks* alone. However, the *Opticks* differs in a number of ways from the *Principia*. It is written in English, not Latin. It is not presented in mathematical form, and does not use mathematical tools to provide proof for its assertions. Instead, the proof comes from the experiments Newton carried out. One of Newton's claims to fame as a scientist is his success both as an experimentalist and as a theoretician. Even Albert Einstein did not measure up to this dual standard.

The *Opticks* concludes with a set of "Queries" that are not limited to the field of optics—the branch of physical science that focuses on light and vision. Instead the queries concern such scientific issues as the nature of heat, electricity, chemical action, and gravity. They also include more speculative matters, such as how God created matter "in the beginning" and how ethical standards should guide human behavior.

Other scientists understood that, in part, Newton's queries indicated his belief that experiment was a crucial source of knowledge. While the *Principia* established the importance of mathematical deduction in securing knowledge, the *Opticks* made a firm case for the importance of experiment as well.

PROFESSIONAL CONTROVERSIES

In addition to his conflicts with Robert Hooke, Newton had several other strained professional relationships. Issues regarding Flamsteed's *Historia Coelestis*—that is, *History of the Heavens*—constituted "the most unpleasant episode of Newton's life,"[19] which reflected badly on Newton's character. Flamsteed's book, an ambitious catalogue of astronomical data, was based on observations he made at the Royal Observatory in Greenwich, a borough of London.

Newton put his own scholarly needs ahead of Flamsteed's. He needed Flamsteed's data on the motions of the moon and planets for a second edition of the *Principia*. Newton was frustrated when Flamsteed withheld his data before the star catalogue's publication, not wanting to release it until he had completed the catalogue.

Newton tried to force Flamsteed to publish the catalogue immediately. As president of the Royal Society, Newton appointed himself the head of a commission to determine which of Flamsteed's papers were worthy of publication. In this role, he ordered Flamsteed to appear at a dinner of the commissioners with samples of his work

The first working reflecting telescope, invented by Newton in 1668, stands in front of a sketch of the device in Newton's Principia.

for their consideration. In 1708, the *British History of the Heavens*, which was based on Flamsteed's data, entered publication. The entire work, as edited—or, in Flamsteed's eyes, mutilated—by Newton, appeared in 1712. The catalogue included only those papers of Flamsteed's that personally interested Newton. In the meantime, Newton punished Flamsteed for his attempts to block publication by removing the astronomer royal from the list of the society's Fellows. He used nonpayment of dues as an excuse.

Certain that the publication of a second edition of the *Principia* took precedence over Flamsteed's right to his own observations, Newton helped himself to Flamsteed's data. The second edition of the *Principia* appeared in 1713.

Shortly before his death, Flamsteed arranged the printing of the *History of the Heavens* in the form he wanted, including all the data omitted by Newton. In addition, Flamsteed purchased every available copy of Newton's version of the catalogue and systematically burned them.

Newton had an equally bitter battle with the German mathematician Gottfried Wilhelm von Leibniz. By 1675, Leibniz had independently formulated the fundamental theorem of calculus, which Newton had arrived at 10 years earlier. Leibniz also improved on Newton's system of notation. Unlike Newton's method of "fluxions," Leibniz's calculus notation is still in use today. Newton later accused Leibniz of stealing his work.

Had Newton published his work immediately in the 1660's, it would have been clear who had first discovered the theorem. Although Leibniz had seen and taken notes on Newton's work in 1676, he borrowed nothing from it. Leibniz wrote a friend: "Mr. Newton developed it [calculus], but I arrived at it by another way. One man makes one contribution, another man another."[20]

In 1699, Leibniz published two papers, along with the invalid claim that Newton owed him a debt for the invention of calculus.

The Swiss mathematician Nicolas Fatio de Duillier, who had once been very close to Newton, rushed to his defense. He challenged Leibniz's claim "to the invention of the calculus for himself."[21] The conflict escalated. Finally, in 1712, Leibniz asked the Royal Society to judge the matter. This was a serious tactical error.

Newton had the society appoint a committee to review the controversy. Although he boasted that the committee was impartial, in fact he hand-picked each member. He personally organized the evidence and drafted the report. The resulting document cast Leibniz in an unflattering light. Even after Leibniz's death three years later, Newton continued to criticize his deceased adversary. The true story behind this disgraceful episode was not revealed for over two centuries.

Newton died on March 20, 1727, at the age of 84, having outlived all of his adversaries. Shortly before his death, he spoke with great modesty of his achievements: "I do not know what I may appear to the world; but to myself I seem to have been only like a boy, playing on the seashore, and diverting myself in now and then finding a smoother pebble or prettier shell than ordinary, while the great ocean of truth lay all undiscovered before me."[22]

Newton was the first scientist to be buried at Westminster Abbey, where he was given a public funeral. A marble monument was erected at the site four years later. Its Latin inscription reads:

> *Here is buried Isaac Newton, Knight, who by a strength of mind almost divine, and mathematical principles peculiarly his own, explored the course and figures of the planets, the paths of comets, the tides of the sea, the dissimilarities in rays of light, and what no other scholar has previously imagined, the properties of the colours thus produced. Diligent, sagacious and faithful, in his expositions of nature, antiquity and the holy Scriptures, he vindicated by his philosophy the majesty of God mighty and good, and expressed the simplicity of the Gospel in his manners. Mortals rejoice that there has existed such and so great an ornament of the human race!*[23] ∎

Chronology of Einstein's Life

1879   born on March 14 in Ulm, Germany

1896   renounces his German citizenship as a rejection of the rigidity that characterizes German education and society

1900   graduates from the Swiss Federal Institute of Technology in Zurich

1902   begins working as a technical expert at the Swiss Patent Office

1903   marries Mileva Maric

1905   Einstein's "miracle year": publishes revolutionary papers on the photoelectric effect, Brownian motion, the special theory of *relativity,* and the conversion of matter into energy and energy into matter *(E = mc²)*

1914   moves to Berlin, Germany; becomes professor at University of Berlin; becomes director of Kaiser Wilhelm Institute for Physics

1916   publishes revolutionary paper on the general theory of relativity, which explains gravity as *distortions,* or curves, in the "fabric" of space-time

1917   publishes "The Quantum Theory of Radiation," strengthening the theory that light exists as *quanta* (chunks of energy); proposes concept of "cosmological constant"

1919   divorces Mileva; marries his cousin Elsa

1922   awarded the 1921 Nobel Prize in physics for his investigations into the photoelectric effect

1929   awarded the Max Planck Medal by the German Physical Society

1932   leaves Germany, where he is under persecution by the Nazi government, never to return

1933   moves to Princeton, New Jersey, where he has accepted a research position at the Institute for Advanced Study

1935   writes paper on the "EPR paradox" with Boris Podolsky and Natan Rosen, investigating the quantum mechanics concept of entanglement

1939   writes letter to President Franklin D. Roosevelt in which he warns that Germany is seeking to develop an atomic bomb

1940   naturalized as a citizen of the United States

1955   signs manifesto urging all nations to stop producing nuclear weapons; dies on April 18 in Princeton, New Jersey

Albert Einstein (1879–1955)

The German-born theoretical physicist Albert Einstein transformed our understanding of the fundamental laws of nature—especially those of time, space, and gravity. Because of Einstein, ideas about the universe that had been taken as "common sense" for hundreds of years were overturned in favor of such seemingly bizarre concepts as *space-time*, *black holes*, and *quantum mechanics*.

The science of physics faced a crisis of confidence in the early 1900's. Scientists had come to realize, much to their dismay, that the theories of Isaac Newton, which had formed the bedrock of classical physics for some 200 years, did not apply to all natural events. For example, Newton's theories could not account for *electromagnetic waves* (waves of energy that make up visible light, ultraviolet light, X rays, and other forms of radiation). Einstein restored order and understanding to this chaotic situation.

Albert Einstein, foreground, *collaborated on a project with J. Robert Oppenheimer in 1947, while both men worked at the Institute for Advanced Study in Princeton, New Jersey.*

In 1905, while working as a young, free-thinking patent clerk in Switzerland, Einstein published four revolutionary papers that transformed physics forever. One paper proposed that light exists as both waves of energy and particles of energy. A second paper provided the first conclusive evidence for the existence of atoms. A third paper replaced Newton's concepts of absolute time and space with the radical notion of space-time, in which space and time are *relative* (changing) and "woven" together in a "fabric" throughout the universe. A fourth paper explained how mass is converted into energy and energy into matter. A decade after these papers, Einstein published another revolutionary document in which he explained gravity as distortions, or curves, in the fabric of space-time.

Einstein's theories made it possible for J. Robert Oppenheimer to direct the development of the atomic bomb. His theories were also crucial for the practical application of nuclear energy and solar energy and the development of computers and other electronic devices.

Today, scientists continue to use Einstein's work to draw new insights into the nature of the universe. Einstein's ideas will undoubtedly serve as guiding lights for centuries to come.

Chapter 1: A Youth of Learning and Imagination

Albert Einstein was born on March 14, 1879, in his parents' house on the Bahnhofstrasse (Railroad Station Street) in Ulm, a city in south-central Germany. His parents were middle-class German Jews who dismissed religious rituals as ancient superstition. When Albert turned 13, he chose not to have a *bar mitzvah,* a traditional ceremony related to religious responsibility.

Einstein's father, Hermann, was a businessman. However, none of Hermann's enterprises—in partnership with his brother, Jakob, or on his own; in Germany or in Italy; in electrochemicals, lighting installation, or plumbing—were successful. Hermann's wife, Pauline Koch Einstein, came from a wealthy family. The Koches were often called upon to help out when Hermann encountered business setbacks. The Koches would also subsidize Albert during his student years.

Pauline Einstein was a woman with cultural aspirations. She insisted on providing violin lessons for young Albert. These lessons began when he was about 9 and continued until he was 13. Pauline's first-born, however, had both a violent temper and a mind of his own. Einstein had other ideas of what to do with his time, and he threw a chair at his first violin teacher, who promptly resigned. His mother was unwilling to yield to Albert's tantrums on this matter. Albert's subsequent violin teachers were so successful that in time his violin became almost an extension of his body.

As an adult, Einstein nearly always traveled with his pipe and his violin. He was never a musician of the first rank—friends with whom he played were embarrassed to tell the great scientist that he was not counting the beats in the music properly. But his love for music remained essential to him throughout his life.

The life of Albert Einstein is the subject of many myths. One story asserts that Einstein did not begin talking until he was 3 years old. Einstein's sister, Maja, who was born in November 1881, when Albert was about 2 ½ years old, insisted otherwise. According to Maja, Albert's parents tried to prepare him for the birth of a sibling by reassuring him that he would be able to play with his new sister

The earliest known photograph of Einstein shows him as a young boy who belonged to a middle-class family of German Jews in the late 1800's.

or brother. Disappointed upon first being introduced to the newborn, he asked, "Where are the wheels?"[1]

When Einstein was in his late 60's, he prepared his *Autobiographical Notes* for a project called the *Library of Living Philosophers*. In the notes, he recalled a magical moment from his childhood that was perhaps the first inkling of the career he would follow: ". . . as a child of four or five years . . . my father showed me a compass. That this needle behaved in such a determined way did not at all fit into the kind of occurrences that could find a place in the unconscious world of concepts. . . . I can still remember—or at least believe I can remember—that this experience made a deep and lasting impression upon me. Something deeply hidden had to be behind things."[2]

His fascination with the forces of nature, however, was not enough to make him a good student. At his public elementary school in Munich, where the Einsteins had moved when Albert was 1 year old, he excelled at math and Latin. But Albert bristled at the expectation that students would memorize material and repeat it verbatim. To his mind, such rigidity not only characterized German education but also pervaded German life. His youthful rejection of such rigidity ultimately led Einstein to renounce his German citizenship in 1896, shortly before he turned 17.

Fortunately, there were other opportunities for intellectual stimulation. His mostly nonreligious parents did observe the Jewish custom of providing hospitality to older Jewish students studying in the community. From about 1889 to 1894, Thursday lunches were a high point of the week for Einstein. Medical student Max Talmud (later called Max Talmey) conversed with his young host as he would with a person his own age. They talked about the scientific discoveries of the day and current "hot topics" in philosophy and mathematics. Talmud recommended books to help Einstein explore these subjects in greater depth, such as the writings of German philosopher Immanuel Kant.

Among Kant's intriguing theories was the idea that time and space are mental constructions rather than independent features of reality. Einstein's own theories would one day transform the conventional views of space and time. Talmud later recalled: "In all these years I never saw him reading any light literature. Nor did I ever see him in the company of other boys of his age."[3]

Albert's uncle Jakob was another frequent lunchtime guest. He introduced Albert to algebra, describing it to his nephew as "a merry science in which we go hunting for a little animal whose name we don't know. So we call it X. When we bag the game we give it the right name."[4] Einstein recalled from the perspective of his late 60's that geometry had an even stronger influence on him: "At the age of twelve I experienced a second wonder of a totally different nature— in a little book dealing with Euclidean plane geometry, which came into my hands at the beginning of a school year. Here were assertions, as for example the intersection of the three attitudes of a triangle at one point, that—though by no means evident—could nevertheless be proved with such certainty that any doubt appeared to be out of the question. This lucidity and certainty made an indescribable impression upon me."[5]

Also at the age of 12, Einstein entered *gymnasium*—the term used in Europe for a secondary school that prepared students for university. He was the only Jew in his class. The state required religious education for graduation, and a distant relative with knowledge of Judaism instructed Albert. Einstein became deeply religious for a year. In this respect, he resembled Danish physicist Niels Bohr, who was later Einstein's colleague and intellectual sparring partner. As a teenager, Bohr also went through a brief period of religious commitment. (In Bohr's case the religion was Christianity in the form of Lutheranism, though he was the son of a Jewish mother.)

Einstein later recalled how his fling with religion ended: "Through the reading of popular scientific books I soon reached the conviction that much in the stories of the Bible could not be true. The consequence was . . . the impression that youth is intentionally being deceived by the state through lies; it was a crushing impression. Suspicion against every kind of authority grew out of this experience. . . ."[6]

Nonetheless, he remained in some sense a religious man throughout his life. When asked about his religious views, he once offered this perspective: "A knowledge of the existence of something we cannot penetrate, our perceptions of the profoundest reason and the most radiant beauty, which only in their most primitive forms are accessible to our minds—it is this knowledge and this emotion that constitute true religiosity; in this sense, and in this alone, I am a deeply religious man."[7]

Einstein's parents trained him in self-reliance from early boyhood. Even before he was 4 years old, he was allowed to negotiate the streets of Munich on his own. Nevertheless, 15-year-old Albert was not as independent as his parents hoped. In 1894, he was left behind in Munich to finish school, while his parents and Maja moved to Italy in another attempt to revive Hermann's business fortunes. Living alone in a boardinghouse, without close friends in school, Einstein felt abandoned. He was resourceful enough, however, to plan an exit strategy. He procured two letters—one from the family physician and one from a math teacher—that convinced the head of the gymnasium to allow him to leave school and Germany. The physician argued that to avoid a mental breakdown, Einstein must be permitted to rejoin his family. The math teacher noted that Einstein had already covered the school's entire math curriculum. In spring 1895, he dropped out of school and left Germany for Italy.

FROM HIGH SCHOOL DROPOUT TO POLYTECHNIC STUDENT (1895–1896)

Worried that his son would be unemployable without a diploma, Hermann convinced his son to apply to technical college. Albert not only agreed but also decided to aim high. He sought admission to the prestigious Swiss Federal Institute of Technology in Zurich—the Zurich Polytechnic, or Poly, for short. The Poly did not require a high school diploma for admission. Applicants simply needed to pass the entrance examination.

Einstein, front row at left, poses with some of his high school classmates in Aarau, Switzerland, where he thrived in an educational environment that encouraged creative thinking.

The test was a challenge for Einstein. In fall 1895, he failed to get sufficiently high marks in the French, chemistry, and biology sections of the exam. However, all was not lost. His application stood out for two reasons. Unlike most of those taking the exam, Einstein was only 16, not 18 or older. In addition, his scores on math and physics were so impressive that the physics professor at the Poly invited Einstein to attend his lectures. The director of the Poly promised Einstein a place in the incoming class for the following fall without a second examination. He would, however, have to spend the intervening year earning a high school diploma.

The Einsteins sent Albert to a high school in Aarau, a small town in a valley 25 miles (40 kilometers) west of Zurich. The local language was German, so Einstein, whose linguistic abilities were not among his strongest, would not have to overcome the language hurdle. Jost Winteler, a teacher of history and classical literature, and his wife, Pauline, offered Einstein room and board and a ready-made family of four brothers and three sisters. Einstein's Koch relatives paid for his expenses.

Although Einstein's time in Aarau was brief, it was significant in terms of his social development and educational growth. One of the

Winteler daughters, Marie, became his first serious romantic interest. He blossomed in a school environment that emphasized creative thinking. At school, and in the Winteler home, controversial topics were open for discussion.

Einstein focused on several subjects in Aarau, including French, which had challenged him on the Poly entrance exam. For a classroom exercise, students were asked to describe their "projets d'avenir"—future projects. Einstein's essay included an explanation of why he wished first to study and then to teach theoretical math and physics. Although his French was less than perfect, as translated, his explanation for these career choices is interesting: "Above all, it is [my] disposition for abstract and mathematical thought, [my] lack of imagination and practical ability . . . one always likes to do the things for which one has ability. Then there is also a certain independence in the scientific profession which I like a great deal."[8]

While young Albert thought he lacked imagination, he had in fact already begun to visualize an image that would lead to his *special theory of relativity.* In his *Autobiographical Notes,* Einstein recalled: "After ten years of reflection such a [universal] principle resulted from a paradox upon which I had already hit at the age of sixteen: If I pursue a beam of light with the velocity c (velocity of light in a vacuum), I should observe such a beam of light as an electromagnetic field at rest though spatially oscillating. . . . From the very beginning it appeared to me intuitively clear that, judged from the standpoint of such an observer, everything would have to happen according to the same laws as for an observer who, relative to the earth, was at rest. For how should the first observer know, or be able to determine, that he is in a state of fast uniform motion? One sees that in this paradox the germ of the special relativity theory is already contained."[9]

At age 16, Einstein was familiar with the work of the Scottish physicist James Clerk Maxwell. In the late 1800's, Maxwell—perhaps the only physical scientist in history whose brilliance equalled that of Newton and Einstein—had shown that light is a wave of oscillating electric and magnetic fields traveling at high speed. Einstein showed a precocious understanding of Maxwell's theories.

Einstein achieved high grades in math and physics and lower grades in French and other classes. On the Aarau grading scale of 1 to 6, 6 is the highest grade. Some Einstein scholars had assumed that 6 was the lowest possible grade, and thus mistakenly concluded that his scores were poor. Albert scored a 6 in algebra, geometry, and history, and a 5/6 in physics. He achieved a grade of 4/5 in German and a 5 in natural history. He scored a respectable 4 in art, technical drawing, and geography, and a 3/4 in French. In fall 1896, Einstein was awarded a high school diploma—his entry ticket to the Poly.

AT THE POLY (1896–1900)

By the time Einstein enrolled at the Poly, he was no longer a social misfit. He was a witty, charming, and attractive young man. Of the four students who enrolled at the Poly along with Einstein that fall, three were men and one was a woman. Before the school year was out, Einstein stopped writing Marie Winteler, his love interest in Aarau. To the amazement of his male friends, Einstein had become interested in their female classmate, Mileva Maric. She was a Serb, four years Einstein's senior, who refused to yield to the prejudice that kept women from studying physics.

Mileva and Albert exchanged a number of letters between 1897 and 1903. In time, they dropped the formalities of speech—he no longer called her "Fraulein" (Miss), she no longer called him "Herr Einstein" (Mr. Einstein)—for endearing nicknames like "Johnnie" and "Dollie," "sweetheart," and "kitten." During this period, their relationship grew from classmates to lovers to newlyweds. Based on some references in their letters to "our work,"[10] some researchers have argued that Mileva was a significant but unacknowledged contributor to Einstein's papers. Most serious Einstein scholars, however, find no evidence to support this assertion.

However, Einstein made one friendship at the Poly that changed the course of his career. From the beginning of his days at the school—and to the great disappointment of the physics professor whom Einstein had impressed with his performance on the entrance examination—Einstein rarely attended lectures in math or physics. He was able to pass these courses thanks to the excellent notes of

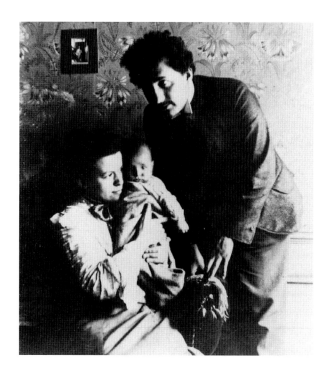

Einstein and his wife, Mileva, show off their newborn son, Hans Albert, in 1904. Another son, Eduard, was born in 1910.

his classmate Marcel Grossmann, who kindly lent them to Einstein before examinations. Einstein later acknowledged how important these notes were to his school career. Grossmann's help allowed Albert to spend his time in the library or the laboratory, reading about subjects he deemed important or becoming acquainted with and "fascinated by the direct contact with observation."[11]

Einstein's intellectual development was strongly influenced by another friendship forged during the Poly period. Around 1897, Albert met Michelangelo (called Michele) Besso, an Italian engineering student six years his senior, while playing music in a private home. Their friendship would last a lifetime. Besso introduced Einstein to the work of Ernst Mach, whose *Science of Mechanics* argued that Newton's concepts of "absolute space" and "absolute time" were meaningless because they could not be defined in terms of observable quantities or processes. Einstein later reflected that Mach's "writings had great influence on my development. But how much he influenced my life's work it is impossible for me to fathom."[12]

In his independent studies, Einstein found that a number of scientists were questioning Newton's view of the universe. He also read the work of German physicist Gustav Kirchhoff, who viewed Newton's ideas as convenient interpretations for a variety of unrelated phenomena. Einstein was especially interested in the work of James Clerk Maxwell. Although Newton claimed that light consisted of "corpuscles" or particles, Maxwell showed that light could also be understood as a wave. His theory of electricity and magnetism proved that light is an *electromagnetic wave* traveling at 186,282 miles (299,792 kilometers) per second. (Electromagnetic waves are patterns of electric and magnetic fields generated by accelerating electric charges.) Maxwell's predictions inspired other scientists to conduct experiments to measure the speed of light.

Despite his poor attendance record and the disrespect he often showed his professors, Einstein earned his diploma in summer 1900. Of the five students in his class, he had the second worst examination scores—just ahead of Mileva, who failed to graduate. Einstein was now qualified to teach math and science on the secondary level, but he had higher aspirations. He wanted to earn a doctorate from the University of Zurich.

POSTGRADUATE SETBACKS AND ACHIEVEMENTS

To obtain his degree, Einstein needed to write a doctoral thesis. He hoped to support himself by working as an assistant to one of the Poly's professors. However, the few available jobs went to graduates who had the best exam scores and who treated the professors with more respect. Albert had to find other means to support himself, especially because he was determined to marry Mileva. In addition, his Koch relatives withdrew the support they had provided him during his student years. They believed that, as a Polytechnic graduate, Einstein should now be able to earn his own living.

Einstein's parents were not pleased that their unemployed son was planning to marry. However, when it began to appear that, despite Einstein's sincere efforts, he really could not obtain a position, his father, Hermann, secretly wrote to Leipzig physical chemist Wilhelm Ostwald. Hermann received no response. Ironically, Ostwald, who would win a Nobel Prize in chemistry in 1909, became, in 1910, the first person to nominate Einstein for the Nobel Prize in physics.

During 1901, Albert supported himself through private tutoring and two temporary high school teaching positions. Late in the year, his Poly friend Marcel Grossmann again came to Albert's rescue. Marcel's father was a friend of the director of the Swiss patent office, from whom he learned that a position would become available in December. He recommended that Einstein apply for the job as soon as it was advertised. In early 1901, Einstein had become a Swiss citizen, which made him eligible for such a civil service position. He interviewed and, in June 1902, won the position—technical expert third class—on a temporary basis. The appointment was made permanent in September 1904.

In October 1902, Albert's father died at the age of 55. On his deathbed, Hermann gave his son permission to marry Mileva. The marriage took place the following January. The witnesses were two Bern friends with whom Albert had started a book club. At meetings of the Olympia Academy, named for the fictional home of the Greek gods, the three young men discussed subjects ranging from astronomy to literature and philosophy.

By the time they were married, Albert and Mileva were the parents of a daughter, Lieserl. The fate of this child remains unknown. She may have been given up for adoption, or she may have died of a childhood illness. Mileva and Albert would later become the parents of two sons, Hans Albert, born in 1904, and Eduard, born in 1910.

By the time of his marriage, Einstein had, on his own, submitted his first professional papers for publication. The prestigious German journal *Annalen der Physik* accepted Einstein's work. Just as Newton and Leibniz had independently developed calculus, Einstein and American physicist Josiah Willard Gibbs each had laid the foundations of statistical mechanics. But while Newton spent much time and energy trying to prove that Leibniz had plagiarized from him, Einstein gracefully yielded to Gibbs's claim of priority. Einstein learned that Gibbs had originally published his work in English in a 1902 book—the German translation of Gibbs's book did not appear until 1905.

Einstein would recover from this setback with a series of astonishing breakthroughs. Just as Newton had laid the foundations of classical mechanics in a year of marvels during 1666, Einstein was to usher in the modern age of physics with his "miracle year" of 1905. The most amazing scientific career of the 20th century was about to take off—and forever change the way that people think of the universe.

Chapter 2: 1905: Einstein's Year of Miracles

By early 1905, five years after he graduated from the Poly, Einstein had published six papers. As one Einstein biographer noted, "It was a good record for a failed teacher who had ended up in the Patent Office; it was surprisingly little for a man who was about to shake up the scientific world."[1]

Einstein was not on the faculty of a university, surrounded by colleagues with whom he could discuss his work. That did not mean, however, that he was unaware of what was going on at the cutting edge of science. From boyhood, after all, he had read books by and about scientists doing pioneering work. From a letter to "kitten" in late May 1901, for example, we know that "Johnnie" was very excited by the recent work on the photoelectric effect by Philipp Lenard. Lenard's paper—a "beautiful piece" that filled Einstein with "happiness and joy"[2]—led to his first epoch-making publication, submitted in March 1905. (No one could foresee at the time that Lenard would, within the next two decades, be transformed into an ardent anti-Semite and opponent of Einstein.)

From a member of Einstein's book club, the Olympia Academy, we also know that one work in particular "profoundly impressed [him] and kept [him] breathless for weeks on end."[3] This book, *Science and Hypothesis* (1902), by French mathematician Henri Poincaré, posed three basic problems that physicists had yet to solve. One problem concerned the photoelectric effect: Why did a metal surface that had been illuminated by ultraviolet light occasionally eject high-energy electrons? A second problem concerned a phenomenon called Brownian motion: What explained the irregular motion of pollen particles suspended in a liquid?

The third problem concerned the nature of light itself. By 1900, as a result of Maxwell's theories and later experiments by other scientists, physicists had concluded that light is an electromagnetic wave. Scientists believed that all waves travel through a medium. For example, water waves travel through water; sound waves travel through air. Some scientists proposed the idea of a substance called

In 1905, *when this photograph was taken, Einstein worked as a clerk at the Swiss Patent Office while he was also preparing papers that would revolutionize the world of physics.*

the "ether" that filled space, enabling visible light and other electromagnetic waves to travel though it. However, experiments had failed to detect the ether. How could light travel without a medium? By the end of 1905, the unknown Einstein was to propose a solution to this problem and answer the other questions raised by Poincaré.

Although Einstein was isolated from university faculty, he did have colleagues with whom he could discuss his ideas. In summer 1904, Einstein's close friend Michele Besso joined the Bern Patent Office after Einstein alerted him to an open position. Besso's position was a grade above Einstein's, and his salary was higher. Instead of feeling jealous and competitive, Einstein was delighted to have someone to walk with to and from work—someone who could join him, so to speak, on a journey alongside a light beam.

Einstein's position encouraged his independent studies of physics. Evaluating other people's creative proposals for new devices sometimes stimulated new ideas of his own. The job also left him with time in the evenings, all day on Sundays, and even occasionally at the office to think about his own work.

One Einstein scholar pointed out another advantage to Einstein's isolation from the established community of professional physicists: "His thinking had not been influenced by consensus views on the proper way to do physics, on what is possible or impossible in physics, or what is important or unimportant in physics."[4]

MARCH: THE PARTICLE NATURE OF LIGHT

In mid- or late May 1905, Einstein wrote a member of the Olympia Academy: "I promise you four papers . . . the first of which I might send you soon. . . . The paper deals with radiation and the energetic properties of light and is very revolutionary, as you will see. . . . "[5]

What was so revolutionary about Einstein's March 1905 paper? In it, Einstein made clear that he was not a physicist to run with the pack. Everyone else might be certain that light was a continuous wave, but in the very introduction Einstein asserted otherwise: "the energy in a beam of light emanating from a point source is not distributed continuously over larger and larger volumes of space but consists of a finite number of energy *quanta*, localized at points of space, which move without subdividing and which are absorbed and emitted only as units."[6]

Einstein was not the first physicist to come up with the idea of quanta, or packets of energy. A more senior German physicist, Max Planck, had introduced the concept five years earlier. During one of Einstein's temporary teaching positions, in 1901, he had learned of Planck's work. But Planck continued to think of light as a continuous wave and of the quantum only as a mathematical tool. Einstein was the only physicist at the time to propose that light consisted of quanta.

At the beginning of the March paper, Einstein expresses his belief that "The wave theory . . . will probably not be replaced by any other theory."[7] Although the paper offers no proof that light consists of quanta, Einstein uses the particle idea as a way of explaining the curious photoelectric effect. Lenard had pointed out that intensifying the light that bombards a metal surface increases the number of electrons ejected but not the *kinetic energy* of those electrons. This effect had mystified scientists. As one scholar has put it, ". . . it would be as if when one increased the amplitude of [a] wave the effect was not to knock . . . swimmers down harder, but rather to knock more of them down with exactly the same force that the smaller wave had done."[8]

Einstein used the idea of the quantum to explain Lenard's observation. No matter how strong the light source is, all the quanta of ultraviolet light have the same energy. If there are more quanta, there can be more collisions with electrons, but each electron will not have more energy.

In addition to explaining the photoelectric effect, Einstein also predicted a feature of the effect that was verified only later: a quantum of light must have a minimum amount of energy to eject an *electron* (negatively charged subatomic particle). Physicists now understand that a minimum amount of energy is needed to liberate an electron from an atom. If the incoming light has less than this minimum energy cutoff, then no electrons will be emitted.

Physicists were very reluctant to accept Einstein's revolutionary description of light. However, in 1923, American physicist Arthur Compton conducted experiments which demonstrated that bombarding an electron with X rays produces the same kind of collision that occurs between billiard balls. It was not until the 1920's that the idea of the light quantum, which Gilbert N. Lewis named the *photon*, entered the mainstream of physics.

In 1909, Einstein predicted the marriage between the particle theory and the wave theory of light. He wrote "the next stage in the development of theoretical physics will bring us a theory of light that can be understood as a kind of fusion of the wave and emission theories of light."[9]

Einstein's March paper thus anticipated and supported *quantum mechanics*, one of two revolutions that took place in physics during the 1900's. It was not his last contribution to quantum theory. Ironically, however, Einstein could never fully accept quantum physics, which placed him outside the mainstream physics community in the last three decades of his life.

APRIL: CALCULATING THE SIZE OF MOLECULES

Einstein's April 1905 paper was less revolutionary than the others he submitted that year. It provided additional support for a view of matter already accepted by most physicists. With a few exceptions, most scientists believed in the existence of the atom. Ernst Mach, however, whose willingness to challenge Newton so impressed Einstein, never accepted the atomic view of matter.

In his second paper of 1905, Einstein used a solution of sugar dissolved in water to determine the dimension of the sugar molecule. Using more mathematics than was typical of his papers, he was able to determine, as he wrote his Olympia Academy friend, "the true sizes of atoms from the *diffusion* [intermingling of molecules] and the *viscosity* [stickiness] of dilute solutions of neutral substances."[10]

This paper finally earned Einstein a Ph.D. degree from the University of Zurich, a process that was far from straightforward. He had already submitted several dissertations that had been rejected. According to his sister, Maja, one of the rejected dissertations was his paper on the special theory of relativity!

Einstein decided to try again with his April paper. Unlike his previous paper, this work was based not on theory but on experimental work. Alfred Kleiner, the faculty member to whom Einstein submitted the paper, assured his colleagues that "it seems to me that Herr Einstein has provided evidence that he is capable of occupying himself successfully with scientific problems."[11] Nonetheless, the thesis was rejected on the grounds that it was too short. Einstein later claimed that he revised it by inserting only a single sentence. It did the trick—the University of Zurich faculty unanimously approved his doctorate on July 27, 1905. The degree itself was formally awarded the following January.

MAY: BROWNIAN MOTION

Einstein's April paper laid the foundation for his May paper, which is considered the first experimental proof of the existence of atoms. To demonstrate that all matter consists of individual atoms, Einstein made use of a phenomenon called Brownian motion. This jittery motion of pollen particles suspended in water is named for the Scottish botanist Robert Brown. Brown demonstrated that the zig-zagging pollen particles are not living creatures, but no one could explain the perpetual motion of these particles in the water.

Einstein used the phenomenon to prove the atomic theory of matter, which states that atoms in a gas or liquid move ceaselessly and randomly. He based his argument on the fluctuations that occur in the motion of liquid molecules. Then Einstein calculated the motion that would result from collisions between invisible water molecules and the visible pollen particles. He worked out a statistical method to chart the behavior of atoms, predicting the distance that a particle of a specified diameter would move in one minute when placed in water of a given temperature. In 1908, Einstein's French colleague

Jean Baptiste Perrin experimentally verified the prediction, firmly establishing the physical reality of atoms.

JUNE: THE SPECIAL THEORY OF RELATIVITY

Although Einstein played an important role in founding quantum mechanics, many other scientists contributed to the quantum revolution. Einstein was, however, the sole founder of a second revolution, one that overturned previous or existing ideas about space, time, and gravity. By challenging Newtonian concepts of space and time, his June 1905 paper was the first shot in this revolution. Within the decade, Einstein completed his revolution by challenging Newton's ideas about gravity.

Einstein was able to trace his 1905 special theory of relativity back to a single moment of inspiration. In 1924, he described the flash of insight that came to him while visiting Michele Besso in spring 1905: "After seven years [1898-1905] of reflection in vain, the solution came to me suddenly with the thought that our concepts and laws of space and time can only claim validity insofar as they stand in a clear relation to our experiences; and that experience could very well lead to the alteration of these concepts and laws. By a revision of the concept of simultaneity into a more malleable form, I thus arrived at the special theory of relativity."[12]

After his insight, Einstein developed the special theory of relativity in only five weeks. The theory is known as "relativity" because it is based on the idea that "all motion is relative." It is called the "special theory" because it describes the special case of uniform motion at a constant *velocity* (speed in a given direction).

Einstein began by asserting that the speed of light in a vacuum is always the same for all observers moving with constant velocity with respect to the source of light. The speed of light is unaffected by any motion either of the light source or of the person observing the light. In other words, even if you are traveling on a jet plane or rocket, you would still measure the speed of light to be the same as measured by someone back on the ground. Einstein also showed that the speed of light in a vacuum is the maximum speed at which information can be transferred.

Einstein used the concept of light quanta to explain the failure of recent experiments to prove the existence of the ether. According to the ether "theory," because of Earth's motion relative to the ether, the speed of light as measured on Earth would depend on the planet's position in its orbit around the sun. In 1887, American scientists A. A. Michelson and E. W. Morley discovered that light travels at the same speed in every direction. Einstein reasoned that if light consists of particles, then it does not need a medium—a light quantum (photon) simply travels through empty space at a constant velocity.

Einstein concluded that the ether does not exist. Without an ether, he said, one cannot define a state of "absolute rest" or "absolute motion." Motion is always measured relative to an observer's position and velocity, or frame of reference. Einstein theorized that in all frames of reference, the laws of nature remain valid and unchanged.

Bern, Switzerland, was Einstein's home when he developed his special theory of relativity, which overturned centuries-old concepts of space and time.

Some of the consequences of the theory of relativity conflicted with common sense. Einstein's theory disproved the idea of absolute simultaneity—the notion that observers will always agree on whether two events occurred at the same instant. The theory of relativity showed that while one observer may see two events occur at the same time, another observer—traveling at high speed with respect to the first observer—would see the events occurring at different times. The special theory of relativity also implies that the rate at which time passes for one individual relative to another depends on how fast the individual is moving. Einstein also challenged the Newtonian view that absolute space exists independent of absolute time. In the special theory of relativity, space and time are mathematically connected, so it makes sense to speak only of a combined "space-time."

Einstein included no footnotes in his June paper. He did, however, thank his friend Michele Besso at the end of the paper. Although it is only 30 pages long, one Einstein scholar said that "in its own way," the June 1905 paper is "as complete as Newton's book-length *Principia*."[13]

The paper was the most controversial of all of Einstein's 1905 manuscripts. Some were dazzled by the elegant logic of Einstein's theory and stood in awe of his creativity; others refused to believe the theory and regarded Einstein with contempt. Nonetheless, by 1911, many leading physicists had accepted the theory's claims.

The special theory of relativity has stood the test of time. For example, countless experiments have shown that nothing can move faster than the speed of light and that the *momentum* (quantity of motion) of an object depends on the observer's frame of reference. Machines known as *particular accelerators*, or "atom smashers," which accelerate particles to speeds approaching the speed of light, regularly verify the theory of relativity.

SEPTEMBER: E = MC^2

Shortly after Einstein submitted his June manuscript, he realized another startling consequence of the special theory of relativity: energy and mass are interchangeable. Just as the June paper brought together space and time, the September paper brought together energy and mass. At only three pages in length, the September paper is the shortest of Einstein's 1905 publications.

Those pages contain an early form of the now famous equation $E = mc^2$. According to the equation, an object at rest has an energy (*E*) equal to its mass (*m*) times the speed of light (*c*) *squared* (multiplied by itself). Since the speed of light is such a large number, the tiniest amount of mass contains an enormous amount of energy.

Einstein's September paper eventually enabled scientists to understand and harness nuclear energy. By the late 1930's, scientists knew that when the *nucleus* (core) of an atom splits in the process of fission, a tiny amount of mass is converted into a tremendous amount of energy. During the 1940's, scientists developed a method of releasing nuclear energy on a large scale.

Einstein's equation is so famous that few people know that he originally framed it differently. He wrote $m = E/c^2$. In trying to understand why Einstein expressed the equation with mass as its subject, rather than energy, Einstein scholar John S. Rigden points to a question that physicists are attempting to answer: Why do the basic particles of matter have their own particular masses rather than some other mass? By 1905, the only subatomic particle that had been identified was the electron, and its mass—though presumed to be small—was not yet known. "Did Einstein wonder, as he finished his September paper, whether perhaps the electron's small mass might be understood in terms of energy, causing him to express his equation in terms of mass and not energy? It would be risky to underestimate Einstein's powerful intuition. . . ."[14]

IMMEDIATE EFFECTS OF THE ANNUS MIRABILIS

The scientific community did not immediately appreciate the magnitude of Einstein's achievements. As the world digested his five papers of 1905, the young patent clerk went about his normal daily life. In the two months following the submission of the last paper, Einstein found it useful to earn some extra money by tutoring a student about electricity. Although he had expected that the June paper, in particular, would stimulate immediate interest, he had to wait until 1906 for any significant response to his special theory of relativity.

What would eventually be recognized as one of the most remarkable years in the history of science ended without any significant change in Einstein's life. He resigned from the patent office on July 6, 1909, and then moved on to take up his first academic position. Even then, his title was associate—not full—professor at the University of Zurich. His beginning annual salary was 4,500 Swiss francs—300 francs lower than that commanded by Michele Besso at the Bern patent office in 1904.

Chapter 3: From the Special to the General Theory of Relativity

In the 1950's, Einstein looked back on his mid-20's as "the happiest years of my life." He had felt no outside pressure as he worked out the theories that led to his 1905 papers. As he told his younger friend and colleague Leo Szilard, "Nobody expected me to lay golden eggs."[1]

Einstein's intellectual curiosity did not diminish following the publication of his papers. On the contrary—upon completing his work on the special theory of relativity, he immediately began to work on a more advanced version of the theory. In 1907, another flash of insight started Einstein down the long road to the *general theory of relativity*. He later called this insight "the happiest thought of my life." Einstein recalled: "I was sitting in a chair in the patent office at Bern when all of a sudden a thought occurred to me. 'If a person falls freely he will not feel his own weight.' I was startled. This simple thought made a deep impression on me. It impelled me toward a theory of gravitation."[2]

While Einstein had created the special theory of relativity within weeks of his 1905 insight, it took him eight years to work out the details of the general theory. In summer 1912, during a hiking vacation with the widowed Polish-born French scientist Marie Curie and her daughters, he suddenly stopped short and said to her, "You understand, what I need to know is exactly what happens to the passengers in an elevator when it falls into emptiness."[3] In October 1912, Einstein wrote a letter to his colleague Arnold Sommerfeld that described the intellectual struggle he was undergoing: "I am now working exclusively on the gravitational problem. . . . [O]ne thing is certain: never before in my life have I troubled myself over anything so much, and I have gained enormous respect for mathematics, whose more subtle parts I considered until now, in my ignorance, as pure luxury! Compared with this problem, the original theory of relativity [the special theory] is child's play."[4]

As Einstein embarked on his academic career in 1909, his name and his work became more generally recognized and admired. In 1911, he was wooed away from the University of Zurich by an appointment to a professorship at the German University in Prague, in what is now the Czech Republic. The following year, he was appointed to a professorship at the Zurich Polytechnic Institute, where he had been unable to get a postgraduate assistantship about a decade earlier. In 1913, Max Planck, considered the father of quantum theory, and his colleagues succeeded in persuading Einstein to live and work in Berlin, the German capital. The city was Einstein's home base from 1914 to 1932. In Berlin, his prestige was reflected in the positions he held: member of the Prussian Academy of Sciences, professor without teaching obligations at the University of Berlin, and director of the Kaiser Wilhelm Institute for Physics (now the Max Planck Institute for Physics).

Flattered as Einstein must have been by the recognition of his accomplishments and future prospects, he expressed some anxiety to a colleague before leaving Zurich: "The gentlemen in Berlin are gambling on me as if I were a prize hen. As for myself I don't even know whether I'm going to lay another egg."[5]

The hen clearly had another egg to lay. By the end of November 1915, Einstein completed the logical structure of the general theory of relativity. In March 1916, his paper appeared in *Annalen der Physik*, the same journal that published the 1905 papers. If Einstein's achievements of 1905 made his colleagues expect more "golden eggs," his 1916 paper surpassed all expectations. Einstein's general theory of relativity has been called his "most notable and his single most important contribution. . . ."[6]

THE GENERAL THEORY OF RELATIVITY

In April 1921, a Boston reporter asked Einstein to explain relativity to the general public. Einstein answered, "Time and space and gravitation have no separate existence from matter."[7]

From this one-sentence summary, it is apparent that Einstein's general theory of relativity changed the model of gravitation that had held sway since Newton's time. For Newton, gravity was a force

Einstein, standing second from right, attends a conference in Brussels, Belgium, in 1911 with other scientists, including Marie Curie, seated second from right.

in itself. For Einstein, gravity is not a force—it is a function of matter and a property of space and time. In order to describe the details by which gravity affects light and matter, Einstein created a new set of mathematical laws. These laws describe the relationship between the gravitational field created by matter and energy and the motion of objects within *gravitational fields*. (A gravitational field is a measure of the strength and direction of the force of gravity at each point in space and time.)

In many cases, the predictions of Einstein's new theory differed only slightly from calculations based on Newton's law of gravitation. Einstein claimed that his theory did not overturn Newton's laws but only expanded upon them. In a book published in 1938, Einstein and a colleague wrote: "The old theory is a special limiting case of the new one. If the gravitational forces are comparatively weak, the old Newtonian law turns out to be a good approximation to the new laws of gravitation. Thus all observations which support the classical theory also support the General Relativity theory. We regain the old theory from the higher level of the new one."[8]

It is said that both Einstein and Newton were led to their studies of gravity by contemplating the image of a falling apple. In 1665, this image made Newton question the range of the force of gravity and ultimately brought him to his law of universal gravitation. Over 200 years later, Einstein realized that, under special conditions, if a falling person dropped an apple, that person would not see the apple fall. Instead, the fruit would hover beside the person. This image led Einstein to his general theory of relativity.

Einstein formulated this thought as a rule that is now called the *principle of equivalence*. This rule, which Einstein developed in 1907, states that the effects of gravity are the same as the effects of acceleration. The image of an apple can help explain the principle of equivalence. Imagine an astronaut in a spacecraft very far from any planet, star, or other object in space that might exert a gravitational pull on it. Imagine, too, that the spacecraft, which experiences no gravitation, is traveling at a constant speed and in a constant direction. In other words, it is moving forward without accelerating. If the astronaut released an apple inside the spacecraft, the apple would not fall. It would remain stationary alongside the astronaut. But if the rocket accelerated by increasing its speed, the apple would seem to fall toward the back of the spacecraft—just as it would if gravity acted upon it. According to the principle of equivalence, there is no physical test that can distinguish between acceleration and gravity.

Einstein realized that this principle suggested a deep connection between gravity, space, and time. From his special theory of relativity, Einstein knew that space and time are mathematically connected. He had already created the concept of *space-time*, which combines time with the three dimensions of space: length, width, and height. (Time is not exactly like the spatial dimensions, though; for one thing, objects can apparently only travel in one direction in the time dimension.) Einstein included gravity by assuming that matter and energy can distort, or change the shape of, space-time. As objects travel through curved space-time, they accelerate—just as they would if affected by a gravitational field. Einstein argued that what we call gravity is therefore not a separate force. It is simply the motion of an object traveling through curved space-time. Einstein is said to have told his younger son, Eduard: "When the blind beetle crawls over the surface of a globe, he doesn't notice that the track he has covered is curved. I was lucky enough to have spotted it."[9]

PREDICTIONS OF GENERAL RELATIVITY

As Einstein developed his general theory of relativity, he realized that it made several predictions that could be compared with astronomical observations. As early as 1907, Einstein saw that his theory could explain the one feature of the solar system that could not be explained with Newton's laws: a tiny variation in the orbit of the planet Mercury. As Mercury revolves around the sun, it *precesses* (wobbles) like a child's spinning top. As a result of this wobbling, Mercury's path shifts slightly with each orbit, so that its closest approach to the sun shifts forward with each pass. When scientists applied Newton's law of gravitation to Mercury's orbit, including the effects of the sun and other planets, they found that the law accounted for most, but not all, of Mercury's motion.

Einstein realized that Mercury, as the planet closest to the sun, travels through a region in which the sun's mass causes a relatively large distortion in space-time. He then used the general theory of relativity to calculate the advance of Mercury's orbit. Einstein's calculation matched the measured advance. This result was the first indication that the general theory of relativity was valid.

In June 1911, Einstein used the general theory of relativity to make a new prediction for astronomers. Einstein determined that, as a ray of light nears a massive object, the curved space-time near the object causes the path of the light ray to bend. Einstein also realized that the bending of light would be detectable during a total eclipse of the sun. With the moon blocking most of the sun's light, astronomers could measure the position of starlight as it grazed the sun's surface. The next total eclipse visible in Europe was to occur in August 1914, in southern Russia. Berlin University astronomer Erwin Finlay-Freundlich arranged an expedition to test the theory. During a famous dinner, just prior to the date of Freundlich's departure, Einstein covered Mrs. Freundlich's fancy tablecloth with equations. She later regretted not having preserved the tablecloth, as her husband had urged her to do, noting, "it would be worth a fortune."[10]

War, however, got in Freundlich's way. Germany started what would later be called World War I (1914–1918) in August 1914, when it declared war on France. Germany's invasion of Belgium two days later brought England into the war. Freundlich and his team were imprisoned in Russia, which fought on the side of the Allies (including France, England, and, after 1917, the United States) and against the Central Powers (including Germany and Austria-Hungary). Freundlich and his colleagues were soon exchanged for a number of high-ranking Russian prisoners of war and returned safely to Berlin.

The delay was fortunate for Einstein—during the interval he perfected his theory and doubled the prediction. Had Freundlich's expedition succeeded, his result would have disagreed with Einstein's original prediction, and Einstein might have been discredited.

The privilege of confirming Einstein's corrected theory fell to English astrophysicist Arthur Eddington. On May 29, 1919, Eddington observed an eclipse at Principe, an island off the west coast of Africa. Eddington's observations showed that light from distant stars deviated from a straight-line course as it neared the eclipsed sun.

Einstein learned of the results of Eddington's expedition only several months later. In September 1919, a cable from a Dutch colleague, Hendrik A. Lorentz, arrived with the good news. Einstein's cool reaction led another colleague to ask him why he showed so little excitement. Einstein answered that he had known all along that the theory was correct. When the colleague asked how he would have reacted had Eddington's result been negative, Einstein responded, "In that case, I'd have to feel sorry for God, because the theory is correct."[11] However, a few days later, Einstein sent a postcard to his mother that began: "Dear Mother! Good news today. H. A. Lorentz cabled me that the English expedition really has proved the deflection of light by the sun."[12]

Later in the 1900's, as technology caught up with Einstein's intuition, scientists continued to verify other predictions of the general theory of relativity. According to the theory, as radio waves pass by the sun, they too should bend. Scientists have measured the sun's bending of radio waves that are given off by *quasars*, which are among the brightest and most distant objects in the universe. These experiments support Einstein's prediction. The theory also predicts that radio waves passing near the sun will slow down. Scientists

confirmed this prediction by measuring a delay of radio signals sent from Earth to the Viking space probes that reached Mars in 1976.

The general theory of relativity predicts that all electromagnetic waves, including visible light, undergo an increase in *wavelength* when they move from a region of space with a strong gravitational field to a region of space with a weak field. Wavelength is the distance between successive crests of a wave. Within the visible spectrum, red light has a longer wavelength than blue or violet light. In terms of light particles, photons of red light have less energy than photons of blue or violet light. According to Einstein's theory, as a photon moves out of a gravitational field, it loses energy and its wavelength becomes *redshifted*. Redshift is a stretching of the wavelengths of visible light or other electromagnetic radiation sent out by a cosmic object.

In 1960, two scientists demonstrated that a beam of very high-energy photons was redshifted slightly after traveling up an elevator shaft in the physics building of Harvard University—that is, after traveling from a stronger region of Earth's gravity to a weaker region. The redshift they measured came within 10 percent of the predicted value. Not to be outdone by their rival, a few years later, a team of Princeton University scientists measured the tiny redshift of sunlight. Their measurement also came very close to matching Einstein's prediction.

Einstein's general theory of relativity led to the modern understanding of *cosmology*, the study of the origin and structure of the universe. In the early 1900's, the scientific community, including Einstein, believed the size of the universe was unchanging. So when equations in the general theory of relativity led to the conclusion that the universe is expanding, Einstein thought his equations must be wrong. To correct his error, in 1917, Einstein added a term called the "cosmological constant" to his theory. In 1922, Russian mathematician Alexander Friedmann solved the original Einstein equations without the cosmological constant. He derived an equation that describes an expanding universe. Although Einstein at first ignored Friedmann's work, and then published a short note casting doubt on Friedmann's result, in 1923, he published a letter admitting that the error was his, not Friedmann's.

In 1929, the American astronomer Edwin P. Hubble found evidence that soon was interpreted to reveal an expanding universe. The cosmological constant seemed doomed. Friedmann's colleague noted that Einstein remarked that the introduction of the cosmological constant was the biggest blunder he ever made in his life. Recently, however, the reliability of Friedmann's observations have been called into question. Furthermore, in the 1990's, astronomers discovered that the universe is not only expanding, but its expansion is accelerating. This finding led many scientists to re-examine the cosmological constant as describing a force possibly behind the universe's acceleration.

Physicists continue to use the general theory of relativity to study the history and nature of the universe. Most scientists believe that the universe began about 13 to 14 billion years ago in a cosmic explosion called the *big bang*. In 1965, astrophysicists Arno Penzias and Robert Wilson, using the new technology of radio astronomy, discovered the "sea" of radiation—called the *cosmic microwave background* (CMB) *radiation*—that was predicted to be a remnant of the big bang. Penzias and Wilson detected low-energy photons coming from all directions of space. In 1992, the Cosmic Background Explorer of the U.S. National Aeronautics and Space Administration (NASA) mapped this background radiation and found it to be nearly uniformly distributed throughout space. In 2003, NASA's Wilkinson Microwave Probe made the first high-resolution map of this oldest light in the universe. Scientists use data from these studies in conjunction with equations based on the general theory of relativity to determine the age and structure of the universe.

Other predictions of the general theory also have been verified. For example, Einstein's theory predicts that waves of gravitational energy should be emitted by massive objects, such as stars, in orbit around each other. By observing objects called *binary pulsars* and measuring the rate at which they lose energy, scientists have confirmed the existence of these gravitational waves.

In 1919, the same year in which Eddington verified the bending of light by massive objects, another English physicist, Oliver Lodge, proposed that this phenomenon could create a *gravitational lens*. A gravitational lens is a massive object—typically a galaxy—lying along our line of sight to a more distant object—for example, a quasar. According to general relativity, the mass of the gravitational lens bends the light of the distant object, splitting it into two or more images as seen from Earth. In 1936, Einstein demonstrated that if a luminous object were located precisely behind a compact gravitational lens, an image of the object would appear as a ring—now known as an "Einstein ring"—around the gravitational lens. Einstein thought the likelihood of discovering a gravitational lens was very small.

Astronomers discovered the first gravitational lens in 1979 using radio astronomy. Other gravitational lenses were subsequently found. In 1987, the first partial "Einstein ring" was detected. In June 2005, astronomers using one of the European Southern Observatory's telescopes of the Very Large Telescope Array in Chile detected a bright, nearly complete Einstein ring near the southern constellation Fornax (the Furnace). To date, this is the most distant

Einstein ring yet detected. Astronomers now use gravitational lensing as the most accurate way to measure the masses of galaxies.

THE GENERAL THEORY OF RELATIVITY AND EINSTEIN'S SENSE OF HUMOR

Einstein had a scientifically ingenious mind, but he also had a delightful sense of humor—even about his crowning scientific achievement, the general theory of relativity. Two incidents from the 1940's, when he was living in Princeton, New Jersey, demonstrate his ability to laugh about the difficulties his relativity theory caused others—and about the trouble other people's work caused him.

In 1946, he met anthropologist Ashley Montagu, who told him this joke about relativity: A Jewish tailor in New York mentions the name "Einstein" to another Jewish tailor. When the second tailor doesn't know who Einstein is, the first tailor says: "He's the guy who invented relativity." The first tailor tells him: "This is relativity: Supposing an old lady sits in your lap for a minute, a minute seems like an hour. But if a beautiful girl sits in your lap for an hour, an hour seems like a minute." Overwhelmed by what he has just learned, the second tailor says: "What? From this he earns a living?"[13] According to Montagu, Einstein said that this joke was one of the best explanations of relativity he had ever heard. (Of course, in fact, the name "relativity" came from the concept of relative motion.)

A few years later, Einstein had a visit from the former major league baseball players Moe Berg and John Kiernan. According to Berg, Einstein asked them to explain baseball to him. Berg got out paper and a pen, drew some diagrams, and did his best to clarify his sport to the great physicist. Einstein grew impatient and said he was unable to grasp what Berg was telling him. As Berg recalled, Einstein served tea and entertained them by playing his violin. He then proposed to Berg the following deal: "My Berg, you teach me baseball and I'll teach you the theory of relativity." Then after a pause, however, the physicist retracted the offer, saying, "You will learn about relativity faster than I learn baseball."[14]

Einstein and his second wife, Elsa are shown in a 1921 photo. The couple were married in 1919. The marriage lasted until Elsa's death in 1936.

Einstein had struggled so mightily in the years 1907 to 1915 with the details of the general theory of relativity that he experienced a serious physical breakdown in 1917, from which he did not recover fully until 1920. By the time he fell ill, his marriage to Mileva was over. From mid-1914 he lived a bachelor existence in Berlin, while Mileva lived with their sons in Zurich. The breakdown was worsened by the conditions in wartime Europe. Einstein's cousin Elsa, a divorcée who lived in Berlin with her two daughters, took care of him during his illness. A few months after Einstein's marriage to Mileva officially ended with their divorce in February 1919, he married Elsa. The marriage would last until her death in 1936.

Although both Einstein and Elsa knew that his efforts to master the details of the general theory had contributed to his physical collapse, he sat back in enjoyment one evening in 1931 to listen to Elsa humorously describe the supposed course of his intellectual journey. The setting was a dinner party at the Beverly Hills, California, home of the motion picture actor and director Charlie Chaplin. Einstein was in California for the second time, as a visitor at the California Institute of Technology in Pasadena.

As Elsa told the story that evening, this is how Einstein discovered the general theory: One morning he came into the living room in his robe. He felt unable to eat a bite of breakfast, however, because of "a wonderful idea." Sitting down at the piano, he began to play, stopping only for an occasional sip of coffee and the repetition of the sentence, "I've got a wonderful idea." The idea, however, needed a little work. Soon he left the living room and shut the door to his study. There he ate all his meals for the next two weeks, emerging only for short evening walks. Finally, one morning he came down to breakfast. Placing two sheets of paper on the table, he announced, "That's it." And that, Elsa told the amused company assembled around Chaplin's dinner table, was his theory of relativity.[15] Of course, it had really taken Einstein eight years of hard labor to craft his revolutionary theory.

Chapter 4: A Celebrity Among Founding Fathers

In early November 1919, the results of Arthur Eddington's eclipse expedition, confirming the bending of light as predicted by the general theory of relativity, were announced in London. The venue was a joint meeting of the Royal Society, one of the oldest scientific societies in Europe, and the Royal Astronomical Society. Over the next several days and weeks, headlines appeared in newspapers around the world, heralding what *The Times* of London called a "Revolution in science—New theory of the Universe—Newtonian ideas overthrown."[1] J. J. Thomson, the president of the Royal Society and discoverer of the electron, announced, "[The general theory] is the greatest discovery in connection with gravitation since Newton enunciated his principles."[2]

The success of general relativity made Einstein a household name, but he did not enjoy the celebrity. On Dec. 9, 1919, Einstein complained to his friend and colleague Max Born that the unwanted attention was "so bad that I can hardly breathe, let alone get down to sensible work."[3] To make the best of a bad situation, he decided to charge a fee for his photograph. Einstein did so not out of greed but "for the benefit of the starving children of Vienna."[4] There was still a lot of misery in postwar Europe.

The public's interest in this remarkable scientist was piqued by Einstein's unconventional behavior. He took very little interest in his dress, for example. Where most other European professors dressed formally, Einstein was totally unconcerned about what he wore, whether the socks matched, or the trousers were pressed. He once said to Elsa: "If they want to see me, here I am. If they want to see my clothes, open my closet and show them my suits."[5] He was equally unconcerned about whether his hair was combed.

Einstein's celebrity had elements of both the ridiculous and the sublime. The Palladium music hall in London invited him for a three-week booking, an offer he found easy to refuse. Lecture halls around Europe and America filled with audiences eager to understand the implications of the new understanding of the universe. The interest was not limited to big cities, either. As Einstein's future co-worker Leopold Infeld recalled: "I was a schoolteacher in a small Polish town, and I did what hundreds of others did all over the world. I gave a public lecture on the relativity theory, and the crowd that queued up on a cold winter's night was so great that it could not be accommodated in the largest hall in the town."[6]

Infeld had an interesting explanation for Einstein's popularity: "It was just after the end of the war. People were weary of hatred, of killing and international intrigues. . . . Everyone looked for a new era of peace, and wanted to forget the war. Here was something which captured the imagination . . . a new event was predicted by a *German* scientist, Einstein, and confirmed by *English* astronomers. Scientists belonging to two warring nations had collaborated again! It seemed the beginning of a new era."[7]

THE OTHER REVOLUTION IN PHYSICS

While the public welcomed Einstein and the new perspectives offered by his general theory of relativity, another revolution was taking place in a different area of physics. The general theory of relativity describes the physics of objects moving at high speeds, huge concentrations of matter, and the evolution of the universe as whole. Quantum mechanics, the other major physical theory of the 1900's, revised classical mechanics as the theory that describes the microscopic world of atoms and subatomic particles. Many physicists in Europe and around the world contributed to the quantum revolution. Einstein recognized the value of both systems of *mechanics*—the branch of physics that studies the effects of forces on solids, liquids, and gases at rest or in motion. But he also believed that neither classical mechanics nor quantum mechanics was complete.

Einstein knew that his theories of relativity had improved upon and extended classical mechanics. Newton's mathematical laws had seemed flawless until Einstein figured out that they hold true only when "the gravitational forces are comparatively weak."[8] Similarly, he could never accept that quantum mechanics represented the most accurate way of describing the structure and behavior of the smallest units of matter. In 1928, British physicist Paul A. M. Dirac was able to develop a version of quantum mechanics that takes Einstein's special theory of relativity into account. But Einstein himself was never able to merge his basic philosophy of science with quantum mechanics.

Einstein's dissatisfaction with quantum mechanics was all the more poignant because, as we have seen, Einstein was one of the founding fathers of that discipline. In 1905, Einstein became the first to speak of the quantum nature of light. Over the next half century, until his death in 1955, even as Einstein insisted he neither understood quantum physics nor accepted it philosophically, he continued to make additional contributions to the field. The importance of Einstein's contributions to quantum theory has become even more apparent in the decades after his death.

Only six years after he completed his March 1905 paper on light quanta, Einstein wrote his friend Michele Besso: "I no longer ask whether these quanta really exist. Nor do I try to construct them any longer, for I know that my brain cannot get through in this way."[9] In 1919, Einstein expressed his inability to grasp what quantum theory was all about. A group of students in Zurich had asked him to lecture on the subject. He told them: "It is not for me to lecture about quantum theory. However hard I tried, I never fully understood it. Besides, I have never gone into the details and tricks on which the quantum theory is at the moment based, so that I cannot give a comprehensive theory. What I have personally accomplished in this subject is easy for you to find out."[10] In 1924, he confided in the wife of his colleague Max Born that his many "attempts to give tangible form to the quanta have foundered again and again, but I am far from giving up hope."[11]

Through his contributions to quantum mechanics and his philosophical objections to the quantum revolution, Einstein defined his relationships with the other leading physicists of his day.

Einstein and his wife, Elsa, attend the premiere of the movie City Lights *with its star,* Charlie Chaplin, *center, during a visit to California in 1931.*

At first, Einstein was not alone in finding the idea of the quantum difficult to accept. Physicist Robert Millikan, Einstein's American contemporary, wrote in his 1951 autobiography, "I think it is correct to say that the Einstein view of light quanta, shooting through space in the form of localized light pulses, or, as we now call them, photons, had practically not convinced adherents prior to about 1915. . . ."[12]

Over the next two years, Einstein wrote a series of three papers that did much to strengthen the theory that light could be thought of as chunks of energy. The last of these three is one of Einstein's most famous papers. Called "The Quantum Theory of Radiation," this paper linked Planck's 1900 work on radiation with Bohr's 1913 model of the hydrogen atom. In Bohr's model, the atomic nucleus is surrounded by orbiting electrons—much like a miniature solar system.

By the time Einstein's paper was published in 1917, Bohr had explained something that had mystified scientists for a long time. Scientists knew that each of the chemical elements was made up of a specific type of atom. They also knew that each element, when heated, could be made to reveal a set of colors that identify it. As physicist Otto Frisch once explained: "Throw a little table salt (or some other sodium compound, like soda) into a gas flame, and it briefly flares yellow; a lithium compound makes it go pink, and so on. If you look at such a flame with a *spectroscope* (a kind of glass prism with a slit in front) you don't see the usual rainbow-colored spectrum but only a few differently colored lines. . . . each kind of atom has its characteristic pattern of lines, its own 'line spectrum,' like a finger print."[13]

Scientists did not, however, understand why each element had a different spectrum. Bohr explained that the electrons in each element are "allowed" to move only along certain paths as they orbit the atomic nucleus. When an electron moves from one orbit to another, it gains or loses energy. The energy is transferred in a single chunk, or quantum. The spectrum of an element is the unique energy pattern of the light quanta its atoms release when they jump from one permitted path to another.

In September 1913, Einstein learned that Bohr's explanation of the spectrum of hydrogen, in which an atom consists of one electron orbiting a nucleus, also holds true for a form of the element helium. Helium typically has two electrons orbiting its nucleus. However, in a form of *ionized* helium, one electron has been lost, leaving a lone electron in orbit around the nucleus.

Einstein was impressed with Bohr's accomplishment: "This is an enormous achievement. The theory of Bohr must then be right."[14] Years later, Einstein complimented Bohr for the "unique instinct" that led him "to discover the major laws of the spectral lines and of the electron shells of the atoms together with their significance for chemistry." Einstein not only compared Bohr's achievement to "a miracle" but also to "the highest form of musicality in the sphere of thought."[15] This was high praise indeed from Einstein, and not only because he loved music. German astronomer Johannes Kepler, whose work was later explained theoretically by Newton, had found the "music of the spheres" in terms of the relative periods of the orbits of the known planets.

In Einstein's 1917 paper, he added to Bohr's explanation. In Bohr's model, atoms give off light *spontaneously* when their electrons jump from a higher orbit to a lower orbit. According to Einstein, light itself could also *stimulate* atoms to emit packets of light.

For many years, Einstein's idea of *stimulated emission* remained an interesting idea with no practical application. Then, in 1954 the maser was developed. The word *maser* is an acronym for *m*icrowave *a*mplification by *s*timulated *e*mission of *r*adiation. The development of the maser led in 1960 to the first laser. *Laser* is the acronym for *l*ight *a*mplification by *s*timulated *e*mission of *r*adiation. Lasers make use of the fact that all atoms of a given element emit specific wavelengths (and colors) of light. When one light particle enters a system of atoms, it stimulates emission, causing two light particles of the same wavelength to emerge. Each additional photon stimulates more atoms to emit light of the same color. In this way, a laser amplifies light at precise colors.

Nobel laureate Charles H. Townes, one of the inventors of the laser, underscored Einstein's insight in the 1917 paper: "Albert Einstein was the first to recognize clearly . . . that if photons can be absorbed by atoms and lift them to higher energy states, then it is necessary that light can also force an atom to give up its energy and drop to a lower level. One photon hits the atom, and two come out. . . . The result is called stimulated emission and results in coherent amplification."[16]

Today's homes, factories, offices, hospitals, supermarkets, and libraries use technology based on lasers. To take only one set of examples, each CD and DVD player has a laser to illuminate the inserted disk. Technologies based on Einstein's own "unique insight" nearly 100 years ago have thus transformed contemporary life in many ways.

EINSTEIN WINS THE NOBEL PRIZE

After nearly two decades of revolutionary contributions to science, on Nov. 9, 1922, it was announced that Einstein had been awarded the Nobel Prize in physics. He had been confident enough that he would eventually become a *laureate* (award recipient) that, as part of his divorce agreement with Mileva, he had promised to turn over all the prize money to her to help support her and their sons.

Einstein had been nominated for the award nearly every year between 1910 and 1922. In 1920, for example, one year after Eddington confirmed the general theory, Einstein received many nominations for the award. No member of the Nobel Committee for Physics, however, approved either of the theory or of Eddington's experiment. One committee member said, "Einstein must never receive a Nobel Prize even if the whole world demands it."[17] Philipp Lenard may also have played a role, by asserting that relativity was unproven and of little value. Rather than give the award to Einstein, the committee decided to give no prize at all for 1921.

The following year, however, an Einstein supporter on the Nobel Committee worked out a strategy. Carl Wilhelm Oseen was professor of mechanics and mathematical physics at Uppsala University in Sweden. It appeared to him that the least controversial piece of work by Einstein was his explanation of the photoelectric effect in his March 1905 paper. At Oseen's suggestion, when the committee voted on Sept. 6, 1922, they agreed to give the 1921 prize to Einstein "for his services to Theoretical Physics, and especially for his discovery of the law of the photoelectric effect"[18] and the 1922 prize to

Niels Bohr "for his investigations of the structure of atoms and of the radiation emanating from them."[19]

Einstein was glad to be able to fulfill his obligation to Mileva and their sons. As for awards, however, they meant little to him. In October 1929, an article about Einstein appeared in *The Saturday Evening Post*. It quoted Einstein as saying: "Decorations, titles, or distinctions mean nothing to me. I do not crave praise. The only thing that gives me pleasure, apart from my work, my violin, and my sailboat, is the appreciation of my fellow workers."[20]

EINSTEIN AND THE UNCERTAINTY PRINCIPLE

When Niels Bohr was awarded the 1922 Nobel Prize in physics, the chairman of the Committee for Physics of the Royal Swedish Academy of Sciences said to him, "Your great success has shown that you have found the right roads to fundamental truths, and in so doing you have laid down principles which have led to the most splendid advances, and promise abundant fruit for the work of the future."[21]

Werner Heisenberg and Erwin Schrödinger were two important contributors to that work. Heisenberg suggested that instead of trying to figure out how electrons move inside atoms, where they could not be observed, theoretical physicists should use such observable facts as atomic spectra to develop mathematical descriptions of atoms. In 1925, he announced one such mathematical description, called *matrix mechanics*.

The following year, Schrödinger developed an easier mathematical description of what happens inside the atom. In Bohr's original quantum theory, electrons behaved like particles. To develop his mathematics, Schrödinger used the 1924 suggestion of French physicist Louis V. de Broglie that electrons could behave like waves. Schrödinger's wave-based mathematics explained not only all the facts of Bohr's theory but also some facts that Bohr's theory had not been able to account for. Soon Schrödinger was able to show that his and Heisenberg's methods led to identical results about atomic structure and spectra even though their mathematical forms were entirely different. The two methods could be used interchangeably. The work of Schrödinger and Heisenberg transformed Bohr's model into quantum mechanics, which was a more detailed theory.

In 1927, Heisenberg formulated an idea called the *uncertainty principle*. He asserted that it is impossible to know at any given instant both the location of an electron and its velocity. Shining even the weakest light on an electron to locate it necessarily changes its velocity. As a result, one could only say where an individual electron was *likely* to be. It would never be possible to predict exactly where an individual electron would be.

Heisenberg claimed that he was inspired to formulate the uncertainty principle by a conversation with Einstein. He remembered Einstein telling him: "on principle, it is quite wrong to try founding a theory on observable magnitudes alone. In reality the very opposite happens. It is the theory which decides what we can observe. . . ."[22] Einstein, however, never accepted the uncertainty principle because he could not believe that natural phenomena, including the workings of atoms, could be understood only in terms of probabilities. He believed the exact properties of atoms should be knowable.

Einstein expressed his rejection of the uncertainty principle in a letter to his friend and colleague Max Born: "Quantum mechanics is certainly imposing. But an inner voice tells me that it is not yet the real thing. The theory says a lot, but does not really bring us any closer to the secret of the Old One. I, at any rate, am convinced that He does not throw dice."[23] Years later he explained his remark to another colleague, German-born physicist James Franck: "I can, if the worst comes to the worst, still realize that the Good Lord may have created a world in which there are no natural laws. In short, a chaos. But that there should be statistical laws with definite solutions . . . laws which compel the Good Lord to throw the dice in each individual case, I find highly disagreeable."[24]

Einstein's search for a *unified field theory* was his attempt to replace the statistical laws of quantum physics with what he saw as the true fundamental laws of physical reality. As one of Einstein's biographers put it, he believed that scientists would eventually figure out "how a non-dice-throwing God had made the world."[25]

A year after Einstein's death, Born explained why Einstein could not make his peace with the new quantum mechanics. Einstein believed that "there exists an objective physical world, which unfolds itself according to immutable laws independent of us; we are watching this process like the audience watch a play in a theater." But quantum mechanics: "interprets the experience gained in atomic physics in a different way. We may compare the observer of a physical phenomenon not with the audience of a theatrical performance, but with that of a football game where the act of watching, accompanied by applauding or hissing, has a marked influence on the speed and concentration of the players, and thus on what is watched. . . . It is the action of the experimentalist who designs the apparatus which determines essential features of the observations. Hence there is no objectively existing situation, as was supposed to exist in classical physics."[26]

The famous Nobel Prize-winning scientist appears on the cover of the Feb. 18, 1929, issue of Time *magazine.*

THE BOHR-EINSTEIN BATTLE

Over the years, Einstein referred regularly to his distaste for a God who threw dice. Bohr would tell him, "Nor is it our business to prescribe to God how he should run the [universe]."[27] The argument between the two physicists went on for years. On at least one occasion, Einstein's friend and colleague Paul Ehrenfest said to him: "Einstein, I am ashamed of you: you are arguing about the new quantum theory just as your opponents argue about relativity theory."[28]

At professional meetings, Einstein would present Bohr with one of his famous *thought experiments*—experiments carried out in his mind. He believed that each one pointed out a flaw in Bohr's system. The most famous incident occurred at the Solvay Conference in Brussels in 1930. Einstein had conjured up a remarkable imaginary device that he was convinced would show that the uncertainty principle was wrong. The device involved scales and clocks. Bohr wrestled with Einstein's challenge for a number of troubling hours. Finally, he realized that Einstein had forgotten to take into account a

Einstein and Nobel Prize-winning Danish physicist Niels Bohr, left, *had a friendly debate for years over the quantum theory. The physicists are shown together in 1930.*

consequence of his own relativity theory. According to the theory of general relativity, a clock that is not influenced by gravity runs at a faster rate than a clock in a gravitational field. Once this effect of relativity was considered, Einstein's thought experiment fell apart.

While Einstein's continual challenges might have annoyed Bohr, they also helped him clarify quantum theory. Sometimes he was able to refine his thoughts simply by imagining what Einstein might say by way of a challenge. In 1948, Bohr wrote a summary of his ongoing battle with Einstein about the uncertainty principle. He concluded by saying: "Whether our actual meetings have been of short or long duration, they have always left a deep and lasting impression on my mind."[29] According to one younger physicist, John Wheeler: "I never heard of a debate between two greater men over a longer period of time on a deeper issue with deeper consequences for understanding this strange world of ours."[30]

Einstein did not reject quantum physics. He believed it successfully explained many things. But he also believed that another, more fundamental theory might eventually be discovered that could describe with certainty how every individual atom behaved. In 1941, John Wheeler tried to convince Einstein that his objections to quantum mechanics were baseless. Einstein responded by saying yet again: "I still cannot believe that the Good Lord plays dice. Of course, I may be wrong; but perhaps I have earned the right to make my mistakes."[31] A few years later, Einstein wrote Max Born: "You believe in the God who plays dice, and I in complete law and order in a world which objectively exists, and which I, in a wildly speculative way, am trying to capture. . . . Even the great initial success of the quantum theory does not make me believe in the fundamental dice-game. . . ."[32]

THE EPR PARADOX

One of Einstein's comments about quantum mechanics, made at a meeting in 1933, has turned out to have surprising contemporary relevance. Einstein asked what would happen if measurements were made on a particle that had interacted with another particle. According to quantum mechanics, certain systems of two particles can become entangled, which means that measurements of one particle's properties—such as its position or momentum—become dependent on the measured state of the other particle. By measuring either the position or the momentum of the first particle, an experimenter could, in some circumstances, determine either the position or the momentum of the second particle even if it were far away.

In 1935, Einstein collaborated with Boris Podolsky and Nathan Rosen to write a paper on the subject. Over three decades later, their paper was rediscovered. They proposed a thought experiment, now called the *EPR paradox* (named for the first letter in the last name of each of the three scientists), in which two entangled particles were separated over vast distances. According to the reasoning of Einstein, Podolsky, and Rosen, if we measure the state of the first, nearby particle, then the state of the faraway particle, which according to quantum mechanics was undetermined—position and momentum cannot simultaneously have definitive values—becomes instantly set. This conclusion, at the time, seemed contrary to Einstein's special theory of relativity, which says that information cannot be transferred at speeds faster than the speed of light. However, a number of experiments have confirmed this weird phenomenon. Scientists now think that EPR is just another example of how our classical intuition fails in helping us understand quantum effects.

Entanglement, a term invented by Erwin Schrödinger in 1935, is today the basis of important developments in *cryptography*—the technology of secret communication. One day, engineers may develop a way to use entangled particles to transfer encoded data over vast distances without the possibility of interception. People might use this quantum phenomenon every time they cash a check or use a credit card. Although Einstein had doubts about quantum mechanics, his ideas on the subject have many applications to technology.

Chapter 5: From Sober Scientist to Political Activist

While the world of physics was enjoying a boom of successful new ideas in the early 1900's, the world at large was in turmoil. These worlds overlapped—during World War I, many physicists had been involved in war work. While Einstein did not participate, he did make his feelings about war known. Einstein felt deep revulsion for war. When some of his colleagues—including the father of the quantum, Max Planck, and the discoverer of X rays, Wilhelm Roentgen—signed a manifesto in October 1914 justifying Germany's invasion of Belgium, Einstein took action. He helped write a second document that argued that there would be no victor in the current struggle, because "all nations that participate in it will . . . pay an exceedingly high price."[1] Despite the document's call "for all those who truly cherish the culture of Europe to join forces" and seek "the continuance of international relations,"[2] Einstein was one of only four signers.

Although Einstein believed Germany was responsible for the war, he was shocked when the Allies showed no inclination to help Germany rebuild after the war. He worried that the peace treaty being drafted in Versailles, France, would punish Germany so strongly that it would lead to another war. A month after the war ended in Germany's defeat, Einstein joined a group of European and American intellectuals who sent a petition to the delegates to the Versailles Peace Conference. The petition begged them to "make a peace that does not conceal a future war."[3]

In the end, the Treaty of Versailles did exactly what Einstein feared it would: it contributed to the start of a second world war. The treaty laid all the responsibility for the 1914–1918 war on Germany. It severely punished Germany by imposing heavy reparations—money and resources that Germany was obliged to pay the Allies for the losses they had suffered. According to the treaty's provisions, Germany also lost all its overseas colonies, and its borders at home were changed to its detriment.

Einstein did support at least one provision of the treaty, however. The Treaty of Versailles established the League of Nations, an international association created to maintain peace among the world's nations. The League failed in this attempt, however, largely because the United States was not a member. In 1922, unable to foresee the League's failure, Einstein agreed to join its International Committee on Intellectual Cooperation. He resigned a year later, when the League proved unable to stop France from occupying the German Ruhr area. France took this step to put pressure on Germany to fulfill its reparations obligations. The invasion, however, helped cause the collapse of Germany's currency. Einstein wrote the committee in anger, "As a convinced pacifist it does not seem to me to be a good thing to have any relations whatsover with [the committee]."[4] Although he rejoined the committee in 1924 and attended five of its seven meetings through 1930, he later described the committee in unflattering terms: "Despite its illustrious membership it was the most ineffectual enterprise with which I have been associated."[5]

Meanwhile, the winds of war began to blow once again in Germany. The National Socialist, or Nazi, Party, under its leader, Adolf Hitler, solicited new recruits by promising to destroy the Communists and the Jews. Unable to rely upon the League to help keep the world at peace, Einstein took other steps. In 1925, he signed—with, among others, the Hindu social reformer, religious leader, and Indian nationalist Mohandas K. Gandhi—a manifesto against required military service. In 1930, he signed the manifesto for world disarmament of the Women's International League for Peace and Freedom. Einstein was also a member of War Resisters International and a director of the German League of Human Rights, which had called for a united Europe since 1914. He did more, however, than merely sign pieces of paper. Einstein intervened to help people in distress. For example, in 1930, he appealed to the Finnish minister of war to pardon a Finn who faced punishment for refusing to fulfill his compulsory military service.

Part of the Nazis' success in enlisting new recruits can be attributed to their accusation that the Jews were to blame for Germany's defeat in the war. This accusation was unfounded: About 12,000

Jews had been killed fighting for what they believed was their fatherland. But this did not prevent the accusation from taking root in people's minds. Einstein had been a religious Jew for only a short period, but he expressed his solidarity with his fellow Jews in several ways.

In 1924, Einstein became a dues-paying member of the Berlin Jewish community. According to one Einstein scholar: "The more Einstein became aware of German anti-Semitism the closer a bond he felt to his fellow Jews. There is no more moving photograph of Einstein anywhere than one taken in a Berlin synagogue in 1930. There he sits—skeptic and free thinker that he was and remained until the end of his life—his unruly hair flowing from underneath the traditional black *yarmulke,* holding his violin prepared to play in a concert for the purpose of raising money to help his fellow Jews."[6]

Although Einstein strongly advocated internationalism over nationalism, in 1919 he became an activist on behalf of *Zionism*— the worldwide Jewish movement that in 1948 resulted in the establishment of the State of Israel. In 1921, he visited the United States with the goal of raising money for the planned Hebrew University in Jerusalem. He told his audiences that Jewish students and would-be faculty members were being turned away from universities in Europe. In 1923, Einstein became the first honorary citizen of Tel Aviv during a 12-day visit to the Jewish settlement in Palestine, and he served for a few years on the Board of Governors of the Hebrew University.

EINSTEIN AND THE GERMAN NATIONALISTS

Neither Einstein's outspokenness nor his Jewishness endeared him to German nationalists. In 1920, an anti-Einstein movement began to grow in Germany. Sadly, many of its members were other scientists, who joined for a variety of reasons. Some resented the fact that so much attention was going to a man who had not borne arms for Germany during the war and who blamed Germany for the war. Others were anti-Semites who found Einstein a convenient target.

The most organized group of anti-Einstein activists was the so-called Study Group of German Natural Philosophers, also called the Anti-Einstein League and the Anti-Relativity League. The group was led by Paul Weyland, but its best-known scientist was Philipp Lenard, who had won the Nobel Prize in physics in 1905. Einstein's interest in Lenard's work on the photoelectric effect had contributed to his revolutionary March 1905 paper on the quantum nature of light.

In late summer and autumn 1920, the Weyland-Lenard group organized gatherings in large halls throughout Germany to denounce Einstein. Swastikas—the Nazi symbol—and anti-Semitic literature were for sale. Along with reporters from major newspapers, including *The New York Times*, Einstein attended the August meeting in Berlin's Philharmonic Hall, where he heard himself and his relativity theory attacked. Although Einstein was seen laughing at some of the more ridiculous things he heard, he felt compelled to object to the meeting in a public forum. An article by Einstein soon appeared on the front page of a Berlin newspaper. In it, Einstein argued that if he had not been "a Jew of liberal, international disposition," no one would have attacked his relativity theory. He expressed his admiration for Lenard's experimental work, but dismissed "his objections against the General Theory of Relativity" as "superficial."[7]

When the press began to publish rumors that Einstein was planning to leave Germany for good, some of Einstein's supporters begged him to stay. Max Planck sent a letter to Einstein, criticizing Weyland for allowing the expression of "scarcely believable filth."[8] The German Minister of Education expressed his hope "that there is no truth in the rumors that, because of these vicious attacks, you wished to leave Berlin which always was, and always will be, proud to count you, most respected professor, among the first ornaments of the scientific world."[9]

Einstein remained in Germany for another 12 years. He hoped that his presence would help the war-ravaged country turn into a better place. He hoped his fame would help conquer ultranationalism, militarism, and anti-Semitism.

As the Einsteins arrived in New York City in December 1930 for a visit to the United States, where Einstein spent the winter doing research, they were greeted by a horde of reporters and photographers.

But he hoped in vain. At a meeting held in Leipzig in 1922, some of Lenard's students handed out pamphlets denouncing Einstein's work as "Jewish physics."[10] In 1933, shortly after Einstein left Germany forever, the Nazi newspaper published Lenard's dismissal of Einstein's achievement: "The most important example of the dangerous influence of Jewish circles on the study of nature has been provided by Herr Einstein with his mathematically botched-up theories consisting of some ancient knowledge and a few arbitrary additions." Lenard went on to blame other German scientists for allowing relativity theory to establish itself in Germany "because they did not see, or did not want to see, how wrong it is, outside the field of science also, to regard this Jew as a good German."[11]

THE DECISION TO LEAVE GERMANY

Einstein still had the appreciation of at least some of his German colleagues. In 1929, he was awarded the German Physical Society's prestigious Max Planck Medal. In honor of his 50th birthday in March of that year, the city of Berlin planned to honor him for service to the city by presenting him with a country house. But his ultranationalist enemies blocked the fulfillment of that promise. Instead, Einstein bought land not far from Berlin, in Caputh, and built a villa there.

As early as mid-July 1922, Einstein began to think about leaving Germany. He wrote Marie Curie: "I cannot stay in Berlin as threats have already been made on my life by the ultranationalists. It is of course difficult to prove whether these threats are real. In any case I shall take this as an excuse to move away from turbulent Berlin to somewhere quiet where I am able to work."[12] After a brief trip, however, he returned to Berlin. There he stayed, hoping things would improve. They did not. In 1929, Lancelot Law Whyte, an English physicist on a Rockefeller Foundation grant to study in Berlin, reported how distressing it was to find that a man so great and world-renowned "had become a symbol for anti-Semitism. His very existence in Berlin University was dangerous."[13]

In 1931, a book appeared in Germany called *One Hundred Authors Against Einstein*. Upon learning of this new anti-Semitic attack, Einstein belittled the idea that relativity could be undone by 100 writers, saying: "Why 100? If I were wrong, one would have been enough."[14] (In 2005, the Max Planck Society mounted an exhibit in Berlin in honor of the 100th anniversary of Einstein's "year of miracles." The literature published in connection with the exhibit included a book called *One Hundred Authors for Einstein,* a collection of essays by scientists who described Einstein's impact on science in particular and on the world in general.)

Finally, Einstein began planning in earnest for the possibility that the Nazis posed a threat to Jews and that he would have to leave Germany. He worked out regular visiting appointments with the California Institute of Technology and with Christ Church, one of the largest colleges in the University of Oxford. A visit to Oxford in spring 1931 suggested he might not be happy there. He reported in his diary how uncomfortable his living quarters were and how irksome he found the formal habits of English professors, who wore tuxedos to dinner: "Calm existence in cell while freezing badly. Evening: solemn dinner of the holy brotherhood in tails."[15] But perhaps America would be more suitable to his needs.

En route to the United States in December 1931, he wrote in his diary, "Today I decided to give up my position in Berlin."[16] However, he was unimpressed with the political conservatism he found in Pasadena. A diary entry after a speech he gave there in February 1932 says, "It is a sad world in which such people are allowed to play first fiddle."[17]

Einstein entered into discussions with Abraham Flexner, an American educator who was to become the director of the Institute for Advanced Study. The institute would be established in Princeton, New Jersey, though it would remain separate from Princeton University. At the institute, Einstein and the other faculty members would have no teaching duties. They would be free to do their own research. Although the idea had its appeal, Einstein did not accept Flexner's first offer. He was not yet ready to leave behind his home, friends, and colleagues.

The Einsteins were close friends of Antonina Vallentin, a foreign correspondent for the *Manchester Guardian,* an English newspaper.

When Vallentin learned that Einstein had turned down Flexner's offer, she immediately urged him to change his mind. Only the day before, the commander in chief of the German army had advised her to tell her Jewish friends to leave the country. He singled out Einstein, because "his life is not safe here anymore."[18]

On Oct. 11, 1932, an article in *The New York Times* reported that Einstein would soon be moving to a new position in the United States. According to the report, however, Einstein said he was not cutting his ties to Germany: "I have received a leave of absence from the Prussian Academy for five months of the year for five years. Those five months I expect to spend at Princeton. I am not abandoning Germany. My permanent home will still be in Berlin."[19]

However, when they left their house in Caputh at the end of November 1932, Einstein told Elsa: "Before you leave our villa this time, take a good look at it. You will never see it again."[20] They sailed for the United States on Dec. 10, 1932, and never again set foot in Germany.

LEAVING EUROPE BEHIND

The Nazis were not the only thing the Einsteins had to worry about as they prepared to leave Germany. For a while, it was not clear that they would be granted the necessary visas to enter the United States. In 1932, a petition to ban Einstein as an undesirable alien had been filed by the Woman Patriot Corporation. This group of American women accused Einstein of being "a Communist and menace to American institutions,"[21] as well as a threat to organized religion. They also dismissed his theories of relativity as lacking all practical importance.

The Einsteins had been to the United States before, in 1921, 1930, and 1931, and had never encountered trouble securing visas. Now, however, they were questioned in the American consulate in Berlin for three-quarters of an hour. Disgusted by what seemed to him an "inquisition," Einstein finally announced that if their visas were not ready by the next day at noon, they would stay in Berlin. He told a *New York Times* reporter that if the United States was foolish enough to deny him a visa, "the whole world would laugh at America."[22] The visas were ready in time for the Einsteins to set sail on December 10, as planned.

The Einsteins' first stop was California, for Einstein's third two-month visit to the California Institute of Technology. At the end of January 1933, while the Einsteins were still at Caltech, the Nazis came to power in Germany. In March, the Einsteins nonetheless headed back to Europe via New York. The German consul in New York warned them that it was unsafe to return to Germany, informing them that Nazi storm troopers had broken into both their Berlin apartment and their villa in Caputh. The Einsteins did not go back to Germany. Instead, they settled temporarily in a villa on the Belgian coast, which served as their home until Sept. 9, 1933. During this stay, Einstein visited England

Music was an important part of Einstein's life, and he especially enjoyed playing the violin, as he is doing here aboard a ship in 1931.

and Switzerland, where he saw his younger son for the last time. His older son later emigrated to the United States and became a professor of civil engineering at the University of California at Berkeley.

In mid-March, the Prussian Academy of Science, which had been proud to invite Einstein to join its ranks in 1913, asked for his resignation. Before the end of the month, Einstein sent his letter of resignation. Following the war he was asked to rejoin, but Einstein refused, explaining, "The Germans slaughtered my Jewish brethren; I will have nothing further to do with them."[23] Historians estimate that the Nazis systematically murdered 6 million European Jews in the course of World War II.

Einstein's months in Europe in 1933 were so fraught with danger that two Belgian security guards were assigned to protect him and Elsa. According to a newspaper read by German refugees in Belgium, Einstein topped Hitler's most-wanted list, with a $5,000 reward (almost $75,000 today) offered for his capture. His photo appeared in a German magazine along with those of other "enemies of the Reich." The caption read, "Not yet hanged."[24]

Cautious and well-protected, the Einsteins survived their visit to a Europe that would be plunged into a second world war before the 1930's drew to a close.

Chapter 6: Einstein in America

On Oct. 17, 1933, the Einsteins arrived in New York and were immediately taken to Princeton. At first, Einstein was not impressed by the Princeton intellectuals he encountered. In a letter to his friend Queen Elizabeth of Belgium, he described the town and its inhabitants in less than glowing terms: "A quaint ceremonious village of puny demigods on stilts."[1] But before the end of 1936, Einstein was able to write to his friend and colleague Max Born: "I have acclimated extremely well here, live like a bear in a cave, and feel more at home than I ever did in my eventful life."[2] (Born had fled the Nazis in 1933 for academic positions in Great Britain.)

After living in temporary quarters for about two years, the Einsteins bought a house at 112 Mercer Street, within walking distance of both Princeton University and the Institute for Advanced Study. Although the Nazis had blocked his bank account in Berlin, he was able to buy the house outright. Einstein had sold one of his important manuscripts on relativity, dated from 1912, to the Pierpont Morgan Library in New York City.

Before he came to Princeton, Einstein's intention had been to spend only a half year there each year. He planned to become both a resident fellow at Christ Church, Oxford, and a British citizen. In fact, when he left for the United States in 1933 there was legislation under consideration in the House of Commons to grant him British nationality. Instead, however, Princeton became Einstein's permanent home.

In May 1935, Einstein made his last trip outside the United States. He spent a short time in Bermuda for the sole purpose of applying formally for permanent United States residency, which had to be done outside the country. On Oct. 1, 1940, Einstein, his stepdaughter Margot, and his secretary, Helen Dukas (who had begun working for him in Berlin in 1928), were inducted as citizens of the United States by a judge in Trenton, New Jersey. (Einstein, however, also maintained his Swiss citizenship for the rest of his life.)

EINSTEIN'S WORK IN PRINCETON

The first change the Einsteins made to their 120-year-old house was to create a study for Einstein. A large table filled the center of the room. In front of a huge window, overlooking the garden, stood Einstein's desk. He did his work there and in his office in Fuld Hall, on the new campus of the Institute for Advanced Study.

Most of Einstein's work at the Institute for Advanced Study focused on a project that he began in Berlin around 1920. He set for himself then a difficult and perhaps impossible task: to work out a single mathematical framework that would incorporate electromagnetism and gravity into a unified field theory. As he described his search in 1929 to a former student, Fritz Zwicky, his goal was "to achieve a formula that will account in one breath for Newton's falling apple, the transmission of light and radio waves, the stars, and the composition of matter."[3] Einstein published his first paper on the unified field theory in January 1922. For the next 33 years, he continued to pursue the elusive formula, until his death in 1955.

As early as 1931, newspaper accounts began to appear claiming that Einstein had reached or was on the verge of reaching his goal. His colleagues learned to take these reports with a grain of salt. One of them, Wolfgang Pauli, wrote in 1932: "[Einstein's] never-failing inventiveness as well as his tenacious energy in the pursuit of [unification] guarantees us in recent years, on the average, one theory per annum. . . . It is psychologically interesting that for some time the current theory is usually considered by its author to be the 'definitive solution.'"[4] In 1946, Pauli was also at the institute. Einstein reported that when he explained what he was working on, "Pauli stuck out his tongue at me."[5]

During Einstein's years at the institute, young assistants came and went, joining him temporarily in the search for unification. At around 9:30 or 10 a.m. on most work days, he would leave home and walk to the institute, sometimes accompanied by his colleague, mathematician and logician Kurt Gödel. Upon arrival at his office, Einstein would work for a couple of hours with his assistants,

New American citizens Albert Einstein, his stepdaughter, Margot, left, *and his secretary, Helen Dukas,* right, *pledge their allegiance to the United States on Oct. 1, 1940.*

reviewing promising leads. He returned home for lunch and worked there on his own during the afternoon. When an interesting idea occurred to him, Einstein would report the good news to one of his assistants by phone. One assistant was Banesh Hoffman, who joined him in 1936 and later wrote a biography of Einstein. Nearly 30 years later, Hoffman reflected on the role he and his fellow-assistant Leopold Infeld played in Einstein's effort: "We did all the dirty work of calculating the equations and so on. We reported the results to Einstein and then it was like having a headquarters conference. Sometimes his ideas seemed to come from left field, to be quite extraordinary. We often had heated arguments, not heated in anger but we were like equal partners."[6]

Although some young physicists were eager to join Einstein in his quest, many more young physicists and nearly all of his contemporaries thought Einstein's search was pointless and pathetic. What impelled Einstein on his search was his dissatisfaction with quantum physics. Since most physicists accepted quantum physics, they could not understand Einstein's problem. When the American physicist J. Robert Oppenheimer visited Princeton in the 1930's, he wrote a letter to his brother calling Einstein "completely cuckoo"[7] for refusing to make peace with quantum physics. In 1947, Oppenheimer became director of the Institute for Advanced Study. The physicists whom he recruited also were mystified by Einstein's dissatisfaction with quantum physics. His obsession with unified field theory baffled them.

Einstein knew that his research isolated him from his colleagues. In a 1942 letter, he confided in a friend living in Haifa, Israel: "I have become a lonely old fellow. A kind of patriarchal figure who is known chiefly because he does not wear socks and is displayed on various occasions as an oddity. But in my work I am more fanatical than ever and I really entertain the hope that I have solved my old problems of the unity of the physical field."[8] In a letter two years later to his old friend and colleague Max Born, Einstein wrote that he was "well aware that our younger colleagues interpret" his inability to accept quantum theory "as a consequence of senility."[9]

His colleagues truly missed Einstein's involvement in their work. Max Born wrote in 1949, "Many of us regard this as a tragedy—for him, as he gropes his way in loneliness, and for us, who miss our leader and standard-bearer."[10]

One old friend who did not dismiss Einstein's attempt to find a unified field theory was Erwin Schrödinger. Although he was not Jewish, Schrödinger had left Nazi Germany in 1933. From 1950 to 1955 he was a member of the Institute for Advanced Studies in Dublin, Ireland. In 1946, the two men, former colleagues at the University of Berlin, began exchanging ideas about unification. Einstein sent him two unpublished papers. In early 1947, Schrödinger believed he had discovered the key to the problem. News of Schrödinger's breakthrough was publicized in newspapers around the world. Upon reviewing Schrödinger's work, however, Einstein discovered to his dismay that Schrödinger had basically plagiarized his work. Einstein concluded that Schrödinger's claim of having solved the problem of unification was an empty boast. In a letter to Schrödinger in February 1947, Einstein suggested they stop corresponding and get back to their independent work. The two physicists exchanged no letters for the next three years.

Although, during his lifetime, most physicists dismissed Einstein's efforts to find a unified field theory, in the late 1900's and early 2000's, some physicists came to believe that Einstein was on to something. These scientists hope to find the key to unification in "string theory." String theory proposes that elementary particles are made up of tiny loops of energy that vibrate like violin strings in 10- or 11-dimensional space. Until a way is found to test string theory experimentally, however, it will remain, like Einstein's quest, only a hopeful approach to a long-sought solution.

EINSTEIN, WORLD WAR II, AND THE BOMB

In the United States, Einstein was at least as politically active as he had been in Germany. The battle to rid the world of the Nazi menace, however, led him to discard his previous commitment to pacifism. From 1933 until after World War II ended in summer 1945, Einstein no longer advocated world disarmament, nor did he encourage young men to resist the call to serve in the military.

Einstein practiced what he preached. During World War I (1914–1918), he took no part in Germany's war effort. On May 31, 1943, however, he signed a consultant's contract with the Research and Development Division of the United States Navy. He told a friend, "So long as the war lasts, I do not want to work on anything else."[11] Einstein's assignment included suggesting new weapons and assessing the strengths and weaknesses of those under consideration. He also put his money where his mouth was. Einstein carefully prepared a handwritten copy of his 1905 paper on special relativity. In 1944, it was auctioned off for $6 million (about $69 million today). Einstein contributed the money to the war effort.

Einstein supported several causes, including the struggle for civil rights for African Americans. In the 1930's, when African American opera singer Marian Anderson was refused a room at a hotel in Princeton, he invited her to stay at his home. He also supported the struggle to establish a Jewish state in Palestine, which became more urgent during the Nazi's systematic slaughter of the Jews of Europe. In 1952, after the death of Israel's first president, Chaim Weizmann, Einstein was invited to become the young country's second president. He declined the offer, explaining that he lacked "both the natural aptitude and the experience" to carry out the "official functions" that the position would require. He added, however, that his connection to his fellow Jews had "become my strongest human bond, ever since I became fully aware of our precarious situation among the nations of the world."[12]

From 1939 onward, Einstein's main political interests involved atomic weapons: the need for the United States to develop the technology to combat the Nazi threat during the war; the urgency of stopping the nuclear arms race after the war; and the defense of those wrongly accused of treasonous behavior related to the bomb.

In late 1938, two refugee physicists from Hitler's Germany, Lise Meitner and her nephew Otto Frisch, realized that an experiment performed recently by two German chemists demonstrated that the nucleus of an atom could be split. Before fleeing Germany, Meitner herself had helped plan the experiments, which involved bombarding uranium atoms with subatomic particles called neutrons. Meitner and Frisch also realized that, according to Einstein's famous equation, $E = mc^2$, the splitting of the atom would result in a small amount of mass being converted into a large amount of energy.[13]

Scientists around the world recognized immediately that *nuclear fission*—as the process of splitting the nucleus of the atom was soon called—could lead to the creation of a new sort of weapon. They predicted that atomic weapons would have much more explosive power than conventional weapons. As one German physicist reported to the German War Office, "That country which first makes use of [nuclear fission] has an unsurpassable advantage over the others."[14]

In summer 1939, Einstein was visited by his younger colleague Leo Szilard. Szilard later reported that Einstein "was very quick to see the implications and perfectly willing to do anything that needed to be done."[15] Einstein agreed to sign a letter to President Franklin D. Roosevelt. The letter, drafted in collaboration with Szilard, explained that the new research might lead to the construction of "extremely powerful bombs of a new type."[16] It warned that Germany might be starting research to develop such a bomb.

In 1941, the United States entered World War II on the side of the Allies, who fought the Axis powers of Germany, Italy, and Japan. In 1942, a special project was set up to produce the first atomic bomb. The project was called the Manhattan Project, because its earliest

The first page of a two-page letter written by Einstein to President Franklin D. Roosevelt on Aug. 2, 1939, warns that the achievement of a nuclear chain reaction may soon make it possible to construct "extremely powerful bombs of a new type."

stages began in the New York City borough of Manhattan. However, the bomb itself was developed at secret sites in Los Alamos, New Mexico; Oak Ridge, Tennessee; and Hanford, Washington. J. Robert Oppenheimer directed the design and construction of the bomb at the Los Alamos site. Under Oppenheimer's expert direction, the Manhattan Project scientists succeeded in developing the atomic bomb before the war ended.

After Germany surrendered in May 1945, the Allies learned that German scientists had failed to get very far with their atomic weaponry efforts. Einstein later said that his biggest mistake was to send the letter to President Roosevelt that led the United States to develop the bomb. He added, however, "But perhaps I may be excused because we were all afraid the Germans would be getting the atomic bomb."[17]

Although the war in Europe ended in May 1945, Japan continued to fight. In August, the United States forced Japan to surrender by dropping two atomic bombs on the Japanese cities of Hiroshima and Nagasaki, killing between 120,000 and 140,000 people. The year 2005 marked not only the centenary of Einstein's publication of the formula $E = mc^2$ but also the 60th anniversary of the dropping of the first atomic bombs. In that year, some letters written by Einstein to a Japanese philosopher were released for the first time. These letters revealed Einstein's reaction to the dropping of the bombs on Japanese civilians. In June 1953, he wrote his Japanese correspondent, "I have always condemned the use of the atomic bomb against Japan but I could not do anything at all to prevent that fateful decision."[18]

He was determined, however, to try to put an end to the spread and further use of nuclear weapons. In 1946, he agreed to serve as chairman of the Emergency Committee for Atomic Scientists. In

October, he wrote an open letter to the United Nations General Assembly. In it, he urged the formation of a world government. In November 1947, Einstein accepted an award from the United Nations Foreign Press Association on behalf of the Emergency Committee of Atomic Scientists. The award honored the committee for "its valiant effort to make the world's nations understand the need of outlawing atomic energy as a means of war, and of developing it as an instrument of peace."[19] The last letter Einstein signed before his death was written on April 11, 1955. In it, he agreed to sign a manifesto to urge all nations to stop producing nuclear weapons.

The U.S. Federal Bureau of Investigation (FBI) documented Einstein's efforts to stop the arms race but never found anything incriminating. However, J. Robert Oppenheimer, Einstein's younger colleague, was not so lucky. During the 1930's, Oppenheimer was friends with many individuals who had been members of the Communist Party. Even though he had directed the successful development of the atomic bomb and had served on the U.S. Atomic Energy Commission (AEC), in late 1953 he was accused of being a security risk to the United States. In December, his security clearance was suspended. Oppenheimer was given the choice of resigning from the AEC or facing a hearing. He refused to resign. During the hearing, many of Oppenheimer's colleagues and supporters testified on his behalf. Although the judges concluded that Oppenheimer had done nothing disloyal to the United States, his security clearance was not reinstated.

Einstein did not testify on Oppenheimer's behalf but, on April 14, 1954, the press carried a statement of support by Einstein: "I can only say I have the greatest respect and warmest feelings for Dr. Oppenheimer. I admire him not only as a scientist but also as a man of great human qualities."[20] Before issuing this statement to the press, Einstein confided to a colleague what he really thought: "All Oppenheimer needed to do was go to Washington, tell the officials they were fools, and then go home."[21]

In May 1954, statements about the Oppenheimer hearings, written by many outstanding scientists, were published in the *Bulletin of the Atomic Scientists*. Einstein's brief statement revealed that in his

Einstein joins a group of other prominent scientists in 1946 to issue an appeal for financing of a nationwide campaign to educate the public about the social implications of atomic energy.

eyes, the real danger to American democracy was the attacks by government agencies on innocent people: "The systematic and widespread attempt to destroy mutual trust and confidence constitutes the severest possible blow against society."[22]

Einstein spent much time over the years speaking out on various political issues. But he never forgot the real passion of his life. He told one of his assistants: ". . . we have to divide up our time . . . between our politics and our equations. But to me our equations are far more important, for politics are only a matter of present concern. A mathematical equation stands forever."[23]

Einstein was hospitalized on April 15, following the rupture two days earlier of an abdominal aortic *aneurysm* that had been detected intact in December 1948. (An aneurysm is a permanent, abnormal enlargement of the wall of the heart or a blood vessel.) On April 17, Einstein telephoned Helen Dukas, asking her to bring from home paper, writing utensils, and his most recent calculations. Dukas fulfilled his request, and the pages of equations lay on his hospital bed table when he fell asleep that night. Albert Einstein died at 1:15 a.m. on April 18, 1955. He died expecting to continue work the next morning on those unfinished calculations for his unified field theory.

Chapter 7: A Legacy of Science and Humanity

The life of Albert Einstein was connected to many scientific and political developments of the 1900's. However, Einstein was also part of the tradition of science that linked him with Isaac Newton, J. Robert Oppenheimer, and countless other scientists past, present, and future. Without Newton's laws, Einstein would never have arrived at his theories of relativity and revolutionized the human understanding of the universe. And without Einstein's theories, Oppenheimer would never have led the Manhattan Project and influenced the political world of the late 1900's.

NEWTON AND EINSTEIN

In his biography of Einstein, physicist Jeremy Bernstein makes some interesting comparisons between Newton and Einstein as scientists. Each man had a so-called "year of miracles" in which he transformed human understanding of the universe. Each was able to make a conceptual leap because each was capable of focusing intensely and single-mindedly on a scientific problem for years at a time. This concentration enabled each man to frame the problem he was considering in such a way that it could be solved mathematically. Each man had deep confidence in his powers of intuition. According to Bernstein: ". . . both Newton and Einstein shared a feeling in the fitness of their own intuitions. As Einstein once put it, 'To him who is a discoverer in this field the products of his imagination appear so necessary and natural that he regards them, and would like to have them regarded by others, not as creations of thought but as given realities.' When a certain point in the creative process had been reached, they 'knew' that they must be right. . . ."[1]

Bernstein also makes an interesting contrast between the styles in which the two scientists presented their discoveries. Newton, especially in the *Principia*, "adopts the rigorous impersonal formal style of a geometry text." Einstein, on the other hand, especially in the early papers, conveys his process of thinking. "We have the continual sense that these papers have been written by a human being, and

that we are witness to his 'personal struggle' with the puzzles and mysteries of the natural universe."[2] Bernstein also notes that Einstein's 1905 papers contain little math. In these pioneering publications, Einstein relies more on "simple thought experiments which enable one to visualize what is going on"[3] before and during the mathematical calculation.

One of Newton's biographers, Gale E. Christianson, points to two additional similarities between Newton and Einstein as scientists: (1) the bewildered reception to their scientific masterpieces, and (2) their failure to achieve their shared goal of scientific synthesis. After the *Principia* was published, even many intellectuals had trouble understanding it. Dr. Humphrey Babington, a scholar at Trinity College, worked his way through the tome for several weeks, only to pronounce that learned men "might study seven years before they understood anything of it."[4] A student passing Newton on the street was reported to have said, "There goes the man that writt a book that neither he nor anybody else understands."[5] Similarly, even many scientists found Einstein's general theory of relativity impenetrable at first. The distinguished American astronomer George Ellery Hale, for example, confided in a colleague, "I confess that the complications of the theory of relativity are altogether too much for my comprehension."[6]

After Newton's death, it was discovered that this scientific genius had performed extensive research in alchemy, leaving "hundreds upon hundreds of handwritten pages"[7] on the subject. Christianson argues that Newton's interest in alchemy had its roots in his attempt to "know everything there is to know about the behavior of matter, from the smallest particle to the grandest star. . . . The great problem is to forge a principle that combines both realms—the vast and the infinitesimal. Newton was the first to attempt it; Einstein was the second. Neither was successful and both men, despite their marvelous achievements, went to their graves disappointed at failing to do so."[8]

According to Christianson, Newton delayed publication of the *Opticks* in part because of his unsuccessful attempt to find a single "unified" principle to explain the behavior of matter. He had intended to publish the book in four parts, but only three went to press. The part he withheld included this statement: "If Nature be most simple & fully consonant to her self she observes the same method in regulating the motions of smaller bodies [including the corpuscles of light] which she doth in regulating those of the greater [the sun, moon, and planets]."[9] Einstein continued to search for his unified field theory until the day he died.

EINSTEIN AND OPPENHEIMER

Oppenheimer had a reverence for both Newton and Einstein. For example, in an essay called "Newton: The Path of Light," Oppenheimer quoted a passage from Newton's *Opticks* in which the scientist expressed his belief in atoms. Oppenheimer went on to say: "Newton saw that what held atoms together and made matter must be forces of inordinate strength, and he never considered their existence without a sense of mystery and awe."[10] In another essay, "Space and Time," Oppenheimer described how Einstein revolutionized "the ideas of space and time, though they go back a long way." He also argued that "it is permissible to think that if [Einstein] hadn't lived, the revolution would not have occurred."[11]

Oppenheimer had begun his career as a theoretical physicist specializing in quantum mechanics. In 1945, the Institute for Advanced Study considered appointing Oppenheimer to a permanent faculty position. However, Einstein believed that Oppenheimer was not the strongest candidate. Together with a mathematician colleague, Einstein argued in a memo to the faculty that Wolfgang Pauli would be a better choice. After Pauli declined the offer, the institute tapped Oppenheimer for the position. Einstein would later praise Oppenheimer as "by far the most capable director the Institute has ever had."[12]

Although Oppenheimer praised Einstein's epic battle with Niels Bohr "to prove that the quantum theory had inconsistencies,"[13] Oppenheimer also felt "sorrow" that Einstein spent so much of his time at the institute devoted to this task. As for Einstein's efforts to combine electromagnetism and general relativity into one framework, Oppenheimer wrote: "Einstein's theory of a unified field remains unsubstantiated and current thought veers away from the universe being built that way."[14]

Following World War II, both Einstein and Oppenheimer worked to slow the nuclear arms race. In 1965, a meeting was held to commemorate the 10th anniversary of Einstein's death. Oppenheimer spoke movingly there about his relationship with Einstein. His words were later reprinted in a volume of essays published to celebrate the centenary of Einstein's birth. Some of his comments in "On Albert Einstein" also apply to Oppenheimer himself: "[A]fter the war, he spoke with deep emotion and I believe with great weight about the supreme violence of these atomic weapons. He said at once with great simplicity: 'Now we must make a world government.' It was very forthright, it was very abrupt . . . still all of us in some thoughtful measure must recognize that he was right."[15] ∎

J. Robert Oppenheimer (1904–1967)

J. Robert Oppenheimer was an American theoretical physicist who became known as the "father of the atomic bomb" for his work as director of the laboratory where the first atomic bomb was designed and built. That designation is ironic, however, because Oppenheimer later worked vigorously to control the spread and prevent the use of these horrific weapons. Oppenheimer shared Albert Einstein's vision of a peaceful world living under a single government.

The development of the atomic bomb would not have been possible without Einstein's famous equation $E = mc^2$, which describes how mass can be converted into the enormous amounts of energy released in an atomic explosion. Einstein's theories were also crucial to Oppenheimer's work in the areas of astrophysics and quantum mechanics. Scientific research today in these areas is continuing where Oppenheimer left off.

EARLY LIFE

J. Robert Oppenheimer was born on April 22, 1904, to wealthy, doting parents. His father, Julius, had emigrated from Germany to America in 1888, to join a successful family clothing business in New York. His mother, Ella Friedman Oppenheimer, came from German-Jewish stock on her father's side. Her family had settled in Baltimore, Maryland, in the 1840's. Ella was a painter who also taught art for a time at Barnard College, an elite women's school in New York City.

According to family lore, Oppenheimer's parents had chosen the name Robert for their firstborn. At the last minute, however, Julius decided to name his son after himself. Oppenheimer's birth certificate

Oppenheimer, right, *at the age of about 6, plays with some construction blocks. His interest in science and technology were evident from an early age.*

thus reads "Julius Robert Oppenheimer." From boyhood on, however, Oppenheimer was called "Robert." When asked what the initial J. at the beginning of his name stood for, he always insisted that it did not stand for anything.

Robert was raised in tasteful upper-middle-class luxury. The family's apartment on Manhattan's Upper West Side was decorated with high-quality European furnishings. The walls displayed an ever-growing collection of French post-Impressionist and Fauvist paintings selected by his mother. From the time Robert was 11 or 12, the family summered at a home in Bay Shore, Long Island. There, he learned to sail.

When Robert was 4, a younger brother died in infancy. His mother never got over the loss. When Robert was 8, a second brother, Frank Friedman, was born. Robert would be his brother's mentor and close friend for many years. Frank's political affiliations as an adult would have an impact on Robert's life.

From an early age, Robert showed deep interest in science. On a visit to his father's family in Germany when he was a young boy, his grandfather gave him a rock collection. Robert became a passionate mineral collector. In New York, his father accompanied him on rock-hunting expeditions. Julius also gave him a professional quality microscope and later found a curator at the American Museum of Natural History to tutor Robert. By the age of 12, Robert had begun corresponding with local geologists. Unaware of his age, they invited him to lecture before the members of the New York Mineralogical Club. The audience laughed when the lecturer was given a box on which to stand. Robert's parents knew their son was out of the ordinary.

Like some other wealthy and assimilated Americans of German-Jewish descent, the Oppenheimers were members of the Ethical Culture Society. Founded in 1876, the movement was intended as a response to anti-Semitism. Its founder, Felix Adler, believed that the spread of intellectual culture would eliminate religious prejudice.

Adler founded a progressive school to "train reformers" who would help make a "better world."[1] Some Oppenheimer scholars have argued that the Ethical Culture School's emphasis on social justice helped shape Oppenheimer's adult political convictions.

The school certainly shaped Oppenheimer's professional future. Decades later, Oppenheimer told an interviewer how important his high school science teacher was in launching his career: "The teacher of physics and chemistry was Augustus Klock. . . . He was marvelous; I got so excited that after the first year, which was physics, I arranged to spend the summer working with him setting up equipment for the following year, and I would then take chemistry and would do both. . . . I don't know what would have happened if Augustus Klock hadn't been the teacher in this school, but I know that I had a great sense of indebtedness to him."[2]

In addition to enhancing his boyhood interest in science, Robert's Ethical Culture School background also imbued him with a love for languages and literature, ancient and modern. Throughout his life he remained passionately interested not only in science but also in humanistic culture in the broadest sense.

EDUCATION (1922–1929)

Robert was admitted to Harvard with the class of 1925. He was unable to begin with his classmates in the fall of 1921, however, because he became ill while visiting Europe with his parents. Robert spent what would have been his freshman year recuperating from what he identified as "trench dysentery."[3]

As one commentator has noted, for both Newton and Einstein, an "unplanned year of intellectual freedom" had "dramatic consequences." The plague years became Newton's most creative period. After dropping out of his German high school, Einstein "read widely in electromagnetic theory" and sowed the seeds of relativity theory by imagining "what he would observe if he were to run alongside a beam traveling at the speed of light."[4]

There is no record of precisely what Oppenheimer did in 1921–1922 while recovering from his illness. He may have done some reading of advanced scientific textbooks, but he himself made no great contributions to science during that time. Under the supervision of his high school English teacher, he spent the summer of 1922 in the U.S. Southwest. There, he learned to ride horses. One of the rides introduced him to the Los Alamos mesa in New Mexico. Los Alamos would figure prominently in his future.

When Robert entered Harvard that fall, he made up for lost time. He took extra courses each semester in order to graduate in three years, instead of the usual four. In June 1925, at the age of 21, he received his degree in chemistry with highest honors. He already knew that his true interest was physics, however. He hoped to continue his studies in England, with Ernest Rutherford, the director of the Cavendish Laboratory at the University of Cambridge. In 1911, while he was head of the physics department at the University of Manchester, Rutherford discovered the atomic nucleus. Soon thereafter, Niels Bohr, then a recent Ph.D. from Denmark who was working with Rutherford at Manchester, significantly advanced the quantum revolution by figuring out why the Rutherford atom was stable. Oppenheimer hoped to make his own contributions to the quantum theory at the Cavendish Laboratory. Rutherford, however, did not accept him as a graduate student.

Robert went to Cambridge anyway. He had been admitted to one of the Cambridge colleges and managed to find work space in the basement of the Cavendish Laboratory. Future Nobel laureate Patrick Blackett became his tutor. But things went badly for Oppenheimer. He wrote his Ethical Culture friend Francis Fergusson, who was at Oxford on a Rhodes scholarship: "I am having a pretty bad time. The lab work is a terrible bore, and I am so bad at it that it is impossible to feel that I am learning anything . . . the lectures are vile."[5] Even in college, Oppenheimer's skills as an experimental physicist had been weak. He was destined, however, to excel as a theoretical physicist.

Oppenheimer had the chance to demonstrate those skills while still at Cambridge, where he wrote two fine papers on applications of quantum theory. His work came to the attention of Max Born, a German physicist then visiting Cambridge. Born invited Oppenheimer to his school of theoretical physics at the University of

Göttingen. There, while completing his doctoral work, Oppenheimer came into contact with the greatest young theoretical physicists of the day. His Ph.D. thesis emerged from the problem that he tackled with Born. The two physicists developed a method for analyzing molecules in quantum mechanics that remains the standard technique used today. Oppenheimer earned his doctorate from the University of Göttingen in 1927.

For the next two years, Oppenheimer held postdoctoral research fellowships at several universities, including Harvard, Leiden, in the Netherlands, and Zurich, in Switzerland. While in Leiden he picked up the nickname "Oppie." In the fall of 1929, he began his academic career with a joint appointment at the University of California at Berkeley and the California Institute of Technology, or Caltech, in Pasadena.

POLITICALLY ACTIVE PROFESSOR (1929–1943)

Oppenheimer was drawn to Berkeley in particular. It did not yet have a program in theoretical physics. While he was in Zurich, he and his colleague I. I. Rabi often discussed the contempt in which European physicists held American physics. Determined to change this perception, Oppenheimer and Rabi each went on to found an outstanding American school for theoretical physics: Oppenheimer at Berkeley and Rabi at Columbia.

In 1954, Oppenheimer expressed his pride in the school he founded: "Starting with a single graduate student in my first year at Berkeley, we gradually began to build up what was to become the largest school in the country of graduate and postdoctoral study in theoretical physics, so that as time went on, we came to have between a dozen and 20 people learning and adding to quantum theory, nuclear physics, relativity and other modern physics."[6]

Although he was a theoretical physicist, Oppenheimer showed his ability to work well with experimental physicists at Berkeley. This skill proved important to his later success as "father of the atomic bomb." Berkeley experimentalists Ernest Lawrence and Edwin McMillan relied on Oppenheimer for the theoretical underpinnings of their work developing a *cyclotron*, or particle accelerator.

For his first seven years as a professor, Oppenheimer paid no attention to politics. He later said: "To many of my friends my indifference to contemporary affairs seemed bizarre . . . I was deeply interested in my science; but I had no understanding of the relations of man to his society."[7] His wealth shielded him from the economic turmoil that affected so many Americans following the collapse of the stock market in autumn 1929. The resulting Great Depression, however, led some Americans, including many of his students, to look to Communism for a possible way to correct the country's social and economic ills. Capitalism, the system on which the American economy was based, seemed to these people to have failed.

In theory, Communism promised "from each according to his ability, to each according to his need"—a far cry from what many saw as the dog-eat-dog world of capitalism, where a few wealthy people seemed to benefit from the labor of their employees. The true nature of Communist rule in the Soviet Union was not yet apparent. Dictator Joseph Stalin not only ruled by terror but also was responsible for the deaths of millions of Soviet peasants who dared oppose his collective agricultural program.

Oppenheimer's transformation into a political activist resulted in part from the rise of the National Socialist, or Nazi, movement in Germany. As he wrote in 1954: ". . . I had a continuing, smoldering fury about the treatment of Jews in Germany. I saw what the depression was doing to my students. Often they could get no jobs, or jobs which were wholly inadequate. And through them I began to understand how deeply political and economic events could affect men's lives. I began to feel the need to participate more fully in the life of the community. But I had no framework of political conviction or experience to give me perspective in these matters."[8]

Three relationships he forged in California provided him with that framework. Most important was his intense romantic involvement with a much younger medical student, Jean Tatlock, whom he met in 1936. Her father, a Berkeley English professor, was one of the few nonphysicist faculty members whom Oppenheimer knew. Professor Tatlock was astonished by how well-versed this young physicist was in English literature.

In 1954, Oppenheimer wrote about his relationship with Jean Tatlock: "We were at least twice close enough to marriage to think of ourselves as engaged. . . . She told me about her Communist Party memberships . . . She was, as it turned out, a friend of many *fellow travelers* and Communists, with a number of whom I was later to become acquainted."[9] (A fellow traveler was a person who sympathized with the Communist Party without joining it.) Jean Tatlock brought Oppenheimer into the world of left-wing politics.

Even before his stormy relationship with Tatlock finally fell apart in late 1939, Oppenheimer had found his future wife. At a party in Pasadena in August 1939, he met Kitty Puening Harrison, who was about to begin graduate school in botany at the University of California, Los Angeles. Thrice married, Kitty also had Communist connections. In November 1940, she obtained a divorce decree and married Oppenheimer the same day.

Oppenheimer's wife, Kitty, waters plants in the family's greenhouse as her husband and children, Peter and Toni, look on.

Around 1937, Oppenheimer became acquainted with Haakon Chevalier, who worked at Berkeley and also had deep Communist Party connections. An incident with Chevalier in the early 1940's would later contribute to Oppenheimer's downfall.

Meanwhile, Oppenheimer's brother, Frank, became a member of the Communist Party in 1937. It was quite common at the time for Americans committed to economic justice to support the Communist movement. Robert Oppenheimer became a donor to numerous organizations, some of which were offshoots of the Communist Party. Soon the Federal Bureau of Investigation (FBI) began to keep tabs on Oppenheimer and his associates. Oppenheimer himself always insisted he never joined the Communist Party, and the FBI could not disprove his claim.

ACHIEVEMENTS AS A PHYSICIST

Oppenheimer never achieved the stature of Newton or Einstein. They remain in a category by themselves, joined perhaps only by the Scottish physicist James Clerk Maxwell for his theory of electricity and magnetism. These scientists were visionaries whose amazing intuitive leaps brought about revolutions in human comprehension of the cosmos. Unlike Newton and Einstein, who had the ability to focus for years on a single problem, Oppenheimer lacked the patience to do so. Nonetheless, during his academic career, Oppenheimer made important contributions to nuclear physics and to astrophysics.

Oppenheimer's first graduate student at Berkeley was an Indiana farm girl, Melba Phillips, only three years his junior. They published a joint paper, "Note on the Transmutation Function for Deuterons." A *deuteron*—a form of hydrogen—is a particle consisting of a *proton* (a positively charged subatomic particle) and a *neutron* (a subatomic particle with no charge). The paper introduced what became known as the "Oppenheimer-Phillips process," which has been called "a nice bit of nuclear physics."[10] According to Phillips, Oppenheimer "was an idea man. He never did any great physics, but look at all the lovely ideas that he worked out with his students."[11]

Together with graduate student Hartland Snyder, in 1939 Oppenheimer published "On Continued Gravitational Attraction." It has been called "one of the great papers in 20th-century physics."[12] Einstein's paper on the general theory of relativity had almost immediately led German astronomer Karl Schwarzschild to consider how gravity would distort space and time when a massive object collapses from its own gravitational attraction. Oppenheimer and Snyder applied Schwarzschild's work to the case of a massive star whose fuel supply has burned out. Their calculations suggested that such a star would continue to contract forever under the force of its own gravity. Not even light waves would be able to escape its gravitational pull.

The paper's significance went unrecognized at the time, which recently led one theoretical physicist at Caltech to suggest: "Oppenheimer's work with Snyder is, in retrospect, remarkably complete and an accurate mathematical description of the collapse of a *black hole*. It was hard for people of that era to understand the paper because the things that were being smoked out of the mathematics were so different from any mental picture of how things should behave in the universe."[13]

In 1952, Princeton physicist John Wheeler chanced upon the neglected 1939 paper. He found its suggestions so intriguing that he focused his research on them. During one of Wheeler's lectures, someone suggested that "black hole" would be a good name for the collapsing star. The name took hold. Since the 1970's, new developments in technology have enabled astrophysicists to detect numerous black holes. Black holes remain a "hot topic" in astrophysics today.

In 1938, together with two graduate students, Oppenheimer also performed significant research on *neutron stars*. A neutron star is the extremely dense collapsed core of a *supernova*—a star that explodes following gravitational collapse. According to one of Oppenheimer's biographers: "Had he lived longer . . . the pioneering work that he and his students did on neutron stars and black holes would have . . . been widely honored, possibly by a Nobel Prize."[14]

After 1950, Oppenheimer published no more scientific papers. By then, he had become a scientific statesman and an institute director.

OPPENHEIMER AT LOS ALAMOS (1943–1945)

Albert Einstein's August 1939 letter to President Roosevelt may have contributed to the creation of the U.S. War Department's secret atomic bomb project. Einstein's famous equation of 1905, $E = mc^2$, was the theoretical breakthrough that allowed scientists to understand the tremendous energy that could be unleashed from the atom. Without Einstein's revolutionary theories, Robert Oppenehimer would never have led the effort to develop the bomb.

In 1942, the Manhattan Project was launched under the direction of Colonel (later General) Leslie R. Groves. Groves knew little about nuclear physics. But having coordinated the building of the Pentagon, he knew how to organize a large-scale project.

Oppenheimer had been doing research on nuclear weapons even before Groves tapped him to direct the secret weapons laboratory that would produce an atomic bomb. Like many other physicists at American universities at the time, Oppenheimer was determined that the Nazis not develop the bomb first. But he was not the most obvious choice for director of the lab at Los Alamos, New Mexico. He had never managed anything larger than his theoretical physics group. Experimentation would be vital to the bomb project, and his personal attempts at experimental work had failed. Groves seems to have selected him because he thought Oppenheimer would not challenge his decisions. He later said, "Dr. Oppenheimer was used by me as my adviser . . . not to tell me what to do, but to confirm my opinion."[15]

Aware of the FBI records on Oppenheimer, Groves nonetheless wrote the War Department in July 1943 to confirm his request "that clearance be issued for Julius Robert Oppenheimer without delay, irrespective of the information which you have concerning Mr. Oppenheimer. He is absolutely essential to the project."[16] Essential he proved to be.

Oppenheimer suggested Los Alamos as an appropriate site for his secret research group. He had fallen in love with the area before he entered college, and he had been leasing a nearby ranch since 1927. Upon discovering how isolated Los Alamos was, some of his colleagues expressed concern. One wondered whether, "if Oppenheimer had been an experimental physicist and known that experimental physics is really 90 percent plumbing and you've *got* to have all that equipment and tools and so on, he would ever have agreed to try to start a laboratory in this isolated place."[17]

Yet between spring 1943 and fall 1945, Oppenheimer managed to do at the remote Los Alamos site what the physicists in Germany failed to do—develop a working atomic weapon. He did so in part because of his charisma—that attractive quality that gives a person authority over large numbers of people. He convinced the most gifted scientists in America, whether recent emigrés from Europe or home-grown, to join him there in a team effort. The goal, he assured them, was more vital to the national interest—indeed to the interest of civilization—than anything they had worked on before or were likely to work on again. Nearly every past and future Nobel winner in the relevant scientific fields answered Oppenheimer's call.

One scholar believes that no one else could have matched Oppenheimer's achievement at Los Alamos: "It was as if all his gifts had been hoarded for this occasion. The all but instantaneous ability to comprehend and synthesize scientific ideas, which had terrorized his students because they could not keep up with him, was now channeled into making the project work. . . . He understood every aspect of the program from physics to the shop, and he could keep it all in his head."[18] This scholar asserts: "if Oppenheimer had not been the director at Los Alamos, . . . for better or worse, the Second World War would have ended very differently—without the use of nuclear weapons. They would not have been ready."[19]

THE "CHEVALIER INCIDENT" (1942–1943)

Just as Oppenheimer took on the most important role of his lifetime at Los Alamos, an incident occurred that would do serious damage to his later life. The so-called "Chevalier incident" began in either late 1942 or early 1943. During a visit to the Oppenheimers' home in Berkeley, Haakon Chevalier, Oppenheimer's friend who taught Romance languages at the university, told Oppenheimer that a third party had approached him. This man, a chemical engineer, wanted to know if there was any chance Oppenheimer would agree to collaborate with the Soviet Union. Chevalier had told the man there was no such possibility.

For many months, Oppenheimer did not report this incident to the authorities. In late summer 1943, while visiting Berkeley from Los Alamos, he made a report to the military officer in charge of security for the nuclear research project at Berkeley. He told the officer that the chemical engineer should be closely observed. The officer reported the conversation to his senior officer, Lieutenant Colonel Boris Pash. The next day, Pash tape-recorded his interview with Oppenheimer. Instead of reporting exactly what happened, Oppenheimer told several different versions during the interview. A decade later, his inability or unwillingness on that occasion to give a straightforward account of the Chevalier incident convinced many of Oppenheimer's critics that his judgment or actions might threaten the national security.

OPPENHEIMER AND THE BOMB (1945–1949)

Oppenheimer's attitude toward atomic weapons began to change as the war neared an end. Some critics took this as additional evidence that he was a national security risk. Oppenheimer was far from the only scientist to experience this change of mind, but—next to Einstein—he was probably the best-known scientist in the country.

Oppenheimer, like virtually all his recruits to Los Alamos, knew from the outset that an atomic bomb would be a weapon unlike any past weapon. That is why they were driven to master the ability to make such bombs before the Nazis did. But within the scientific community, attitudes about atomic weapons and nuclear policy went through several stages as the war progressed and after it ended.

The first stage began with a visit of Niels Bohr to Los Alamos around New Year's 1944. Bohr, one of the leaders of the quantum revolution in physics, had come to believe that a pointless and destructive nuclear weapons race would likely follow the war. Such an arms race could be stopped in only one way: scientists from all countries must share their ideas openly. Oppenheimer was deeply affected by Bohr's statement.

The second stage began when two things became clear: that Germany had not succeeded in launching an effective nuclear weapons program and that Germany would lose the war. Many scientists at Los Alamos wondered whether they should continue to work on the bomb, now that it would not have to be used against the Nazis. Oppenheimer convinced them to continue the work. If the world were to understand the terribly destructive nature of this new weapon, the weapon would have to be demonstrated.

Other Manhattan Project scientists disagreed with Oppenheimer. A group at another division, based at the University of Chicago, issued a report in June 1945. It argued that the United States should not be first to use an atomic bomb. If it did use such a weapon of

mass destruction, the United States "would sacrifice public support throughout the world, precipitate the race of armaments, and prejudice the possibility of reaching international agreement on the future control of such weapons."[20] Oppenheimer, however, helped select the Japanese cities on which the first nuclear bombs in history were to be dropped.

On July 16, 1945, the first atomic bomb was successfully tested near Alamogordo, New Mexico. Oppenheimer later described to a documentary filmmaker the mood after the event: "We waited until the blast had passed, walked out of the shelter, and then it was extremely solemn. We knew the world would not be the same. . . . Most people were silent. I remembered the line from the Hindu scripture, the *Bhagavad Gita:* . . . 'Now I have become Death, the destroyer of worlds.' I suppose we all thought that, one way or another."[21]

On Aug. 6, 1945, the atomic bomb was put to its first military use when it was dropped on Hiroshima, where the headquarters of the Japanese Army defending southern Japan was located. Three days later, when the Japanese still showed no signs of surrendering, a second atomic bomb was dropped on Nagasaki, another city important to the Japanese war effort.

Scientists at Los Alamos felt a wave of conflicting reactions: satisfaction that they had successfully completed the job they had set out to do, but horror at the outcome. An estimated 70,000 to 100,000 people were killed by the Hiroshima bomb. An additional 40,000 died in Nagasaki. Later, more than 100,000 people died as a result of radiation poisoning from the two bombs. On August 14, the emperor of Japan overrode his advisors and agreed to end the war. Japan officially surrendered on September 2. The Allies had planned an invasion for November that might have cost as many as 1 million U.S. lives, but it never had to be carried out.

In mid-October, Oppenheimer addressed the approximately 500 scientists who remained at Los Alamos on his last day as director. He stressed their shared conviction at the project's outset: that the Nazis might produce such weapons first, and that without them the Allies might lose the war. He also reminded them of their shared belief that the United States was the place "where the development of atomic weapons would have a better chance of leading to a reasonable solution, and a smaller chance of leading to a disaster." He underlined scientists' shared assumption that "it is good to find out how the world works."[22] Oppenheimer expressed his hope that all those involved in the project would look back on their accomplishments with pride. He warned, however, "If atomic bombs are to be added as new weapons to the arsenals of a warring world, or to the arsenals of nations preparing for war, then the time will come when mankind will curse the names of Los Alamos and Hiroshima."[23]

After leaving Los Alamos for good, Oppenheimer returned briefly to academic life in California. But in 1947, he agreed to become the director of the Institute for Advanced Study in Princeton, New Jersey. Albert Einstein had already been on the institute's faculty for 14 years. Oppenheimer hoped to make the institute into a place where scientists, social scientists, and humanists could work together.

All that remains of a tall steel tower on which an atomic bomb hung are several rods sticking out of the ground after the bomb was tested at the Manhattan Project's New Mexico site in September 1945. Oppenheimer views the remains with Major Leslie R. Groves.

In the meantime, in January 1946, the U.S. Atomic Energy Commission (AEC) was created. The AEC was a civilian agency in charge of the development and use of atomic energy. The commission set up a General Advisory Committee (GAC) of nine. Oppenheimer was elected the chairman of the GAC. From his new base in Princeton, Oppenheimer was closer to Washington, D.C., where important policy decisions about atomic matters were being made.

By this time, the United States was involved in what became known as the *Cold War.* This intense rivalry between Communist and non-Communist countries developed after World War II. It was characterized by deep suspicion between the United States (and its allies) and the Soviet Union (and its allies). Oppenheimer's Communist tendencies in the late 1930's once more became a cause for concern. In 1947, the FBI sent its files on Oppenheimer and his brother to the chairman of the AEC. After reviewing the files thoroughly, the AEC granted Oppenheimer security clearance.

At the end of August 1949, the Soviet Union tested its first nuclear weapon. Some American scientists believed that the new threat demanded the development of what was called the "super"— a hydrogen bomb. The atomic bomb had been based on the process of *nuclear fission,* expressed by Einstein's equation $E = mc^2$. The "super" was based on the process of *nuclear fusion,* the same process that powers the sun and other stars. In autumn 1949, the GAC, headed by Oppenheimer, issued a report arguing against the creation of the "super": "We believe a super bomb should never be produced. . . . In determining not to proceed to develop the super bomb, we see a unique opportunity of providing by example some limitations on the totality of war and thus of limiting the fear and arousing the hopes of mankind."[24] Nonetheless, in 1950, President Harry S. Truman directed the AEC "to continue its work on all forms of atomic weapons, including the so-called hydrogen or superbomb."[25]

The cover of the Nov. 8, 1948, issue of Time *magazine featured a steely-eyed Oppenheimer in front of a blackboard with a maze of mathematical calculations.*

Soon Oppenheimer's failure to enthusiastically support development of the hydrogen bomb would be used to question his loyalty to the United States. The Hungarian-born scientist Edward Teller was the earliest and most vocal advocate of the "super." He had been at Los Alamos during the war, and after Truman's announcement, Teller returned there to work on the hydrogen bomb. The first hydrogen bomb was tested on a small island in the North Pacific Ocean on Nov. 1, 1952.

About six months earlier, Teller went to the FBI to file charges against Oppenheimer. He accused Oppenheimer of attempting "to delay or hinder the development of the H-bomb." He also told the FBI that, although he himself did not think Oppenheimer was "disloyal," nonetheless, "a lot of people believe Oppenheimer opposed the development of the H-bomb on 'direct orders from Moscow.'" Teller said he "would do anything possible"[26] to put an end to Oppenheimer's advisory role in government policy.

ATOMIC ENERGY COMMISSION HEARING

In November 1952, the Republican candidate, war hero General Dwight D. Eisenhower, won the presidency. His election ended a 20-year-period during which Democrats occupied the White House. Part of the Republican platform was the promise to root out Communists in government. The country was in the grip of McCarthyism. Named for Republican Senator Joseph R. McCarthy of Wisconsin, who accused many officials of Communist ties, "McCarthyism" became the term describing the practice of accusing others of disloyalty, often without significant evidence.

In December 1953, at a meeting in Washington, Oppenheimer was handed a letter from the general manager of the AEC. The letter informed him that "there has developed considerable question whether your continued employment on Atomic Energy Commission work will endanger the common defense and security and whether such continued employment is clearly consistent with the interests of the national security."[27] The letter concluded by informing him that the AEC was suspending his security clearance.

Oppenheimer was presented a choice: to resign or submit to a hearing—a trial of sorts—that would determine the outcome. Oppenheimer decided not to resign because doing so "would mean that I accept and concur in the view that I am not fit to serve this government that I have now served for some 12 years."[28]

The hearings were held in April and May 1954 in Washington, D.C. Teller was among those testifying against Oppenheimer. He said, "If it is a question of wisdom and judgment as demonstrated by actions since 1945, then I would say one would be wiser not to grant clearance."[29] Teller later devoted a chapter to the Oppenheimer hearings in his memoirs. There he wrote: "I was certain that Oppenheimer would be cleared. I thought . . . the testimony might demonstrate the degree to which Oppenheimer's advice was wrong-headed. I went over all the incidents where I felt his advice had worked against national well-being. . . ."[30]

Testifying before the Joint Atomic Energy Committee of the U.S. Congress in June 1949, Oppenheimer presents his views on the Soviet Union's technological capabilities regarding atomic weapons.

The AEC had selected a panel to weigh the evidence against Oppenheimer. The majority of the panel concluded that Oppenheimer was "a loyal citizen" but that his advice with regard to the hydrogen bomb was disturbing. The panel was also troubled by his inability to explain the Chevalier incident. In the end, the panel concluded that they could not reinstate Oppenheimer's security clearance. Only one member of the panel reported differently: "To deny him clearance now for what he was cleared for in 1947 . . . seems hardly the procedure to be adopted in a free country."[31]

In late 1954, Senator McCarthy was censured by the Senate. The political climate in the country would soon change, but Oppenheimer would never serve in government again. In December 1963, however, President Lyndon B. Johnson presented Oppenheimer with the Atomic Energy Commission's most prestigious award. Ironically, Oppenheimer was nominated by Edward Teller, who had won the award the previous year.

A SCIENTIST AND A HUMANIST

After the verdict was published, Oppenheimer was uncertain whether the trustees of the Institute for Advanced Study would permit him to remain as director. The institute faculty rallied behind him, however. Every member of the permanent faculty signed an open letter supporting Oppenheimer. In autumn 1954, the trustees voted to retain Oppenheimer as director.

Oppenheimer spent the rest of his life working at the institute. Declining health led to his resignation as director in 1966. But until his death on Feb. 18, 1967, he continued there as a senior professor of physics.

Toward the end of his life, Oppenheimer campaigned for international peace from outside the workings of government. In 1964, he organized a meeting of scientists and other academics to discuss this cause at Mount Kisco, north of New York City. He began the conference by speaking about his personal experience as a scientist and member of human society:

> Up until now . . . I hardly took any action, hardly did anything, or failed to do anything, whether it was a paper on physics, or a lecture, or how I read a book, how I talked to a friend, how I loved, that did not arouse in me a very great sense of revulsion and of wrong. It turned out to be impossible . . . for me to live with anybody else, without understanding that what I saw was only one part of the truth . . . and in an attempt to break out and be a reasonable man, I had to realize that my own worries about what I did were valid and were important, but that they were not the whole story, that there must be a complementary way of looking at them, because other people did not see them as I did. And I needed what they saw, needed them.[32] ■

Notes

ISAAC NEWTON

1. Qtd. in Richard S. Westfall, *The Life of Isaac Newton* (Cambridge, UK: Cambridge University Press, 1993) 7.
2. Qtd. in Westfall 20.
3. Qtd. in Westfall 27.
4. Qtd. in Gale E. Christianson, *Isaac Newton and the Scientific Revolution* (New York: Oxford University Press, 1996) 36.
5. William Stukeley *Memoirs of Sir Isaac Newton* (London: Taylor and Francis, 1936) 20.
6. Qtd. in Christianson 40.
7. Qtd. in Christianson 41.
8. Qtd. in Christianson 49.
9. Qtd. in Christianson 51.
10. Qtd. in Christianson 56.
11. Qtd. in Christianson 82.
12. Qtd. in Christianson 92.
13. Qtd. in Ronald W. Clark, *Einstein: The Life and Times* (New York: World Publishing Company, 1971) 75.
14. Christianson 99.
15. Christianson 115.
16. Christianson 119.
17. Stukeley 78-80.
18. Qtd. in Westfall 251.
19. Westfall 271.
20. Christianson 134.
21. Christianson 135.
22. Leslie Forster Stevenson and Henry Byerly, *The Many Faces of Science: An Introduction to Scientists, Values, and Society* (Boulder, CO: Westview Press, 1995) 45.
23. Mordechai Feingold, *The Newtonian Moment: Isaac Newton and the Making of Modern Culture* (New York: The New York Public Library/Oxford University Press, 2004) 170.

ALBERT EINSTEIN

Chapter 1

1. Denis Brian, *Einstein: A Life* (New York: John Wiley & Sons, Inc., 1995) 1.
2. Albert Einstein, *Autobiographical Notes*, trans. and ed. Paul Arthur Schilpp (La Salle and Chicago, IL: Open Court Publishing Company, 1979) 9.
3. Qtd. in Abraham Pais, *Einstein Lived Here* (Oxford: Clarendon Press, 1994) 123.
4. Qtd. in Brian 4.
5. Einstein, *Autobiographical Notes* 9.
6. Qtd. in Pais, *Einstein Lived Here* 115.
7. Qtd. in Pais, *Einstein Lived Here* 118.
8. Qtd. in Pais, *"Subtle Is the Lord": The Science and the Life of Albert Einstein* (Oxford: Clarendon Press, 1982) 40.
9. Einstein, *Autobiographical Notes* 49, 51.
10. Einstein, *Albert Einstein/Mileva Maric: The Love Letters*, ed. Jürgen Renn and Robert Schulmann, trans. Shawn Smith (Princeton: Princeton University Press, 1992) 32.
11. Pais, *"Subtle Is the Lord"* 44.
12. Ronald W. Clark, *Einstein: The Life and Times* (New York: World Publishing Company, 1971) 38.

Chapter 2

1. Clark 59.
2. Qtd. in Einstein, *The Love Letters* 54.
3. Qtd. in Pais, *"Subtle Is the Lord"* 134.
4. John S. Rigden, *Einstein 1905: The Standard of Greatness* (Cambridge, MA: Harvard University Press, 2005) 128.
5. Qtd. in Rigden 3.
6. Qtd. in Jeremy Bernstein, *Einstein* (New York: The Viking Press, 1973) 202.
7. Qtd. in Bernstein 201.
8. Bernstein 199.
9. Qtd. in Rigden 131.
10. Qtd. in Rigden 3.
11. Qtd. in Rigden 45.
12. Einstein, *The Collected Letters of Albert Einstein, vol. 2, The Swiss Years, Writings, 1900-1909*, John Stachel, et. al, eds. (Princeton: Princeton Univ. Pr., 1989) 199.
13. Einstein scholar Arthur Miller, quoted in Rigden, 86.
14. Rigden 124.

Chapter 3

1. Qtd. in Rigden 150.
2. Qtd. in Rigden, 5.
3. Qtd. in Brian 86.
4. Qtd. in Rigden 6.
5. Qtd. in Clark 173.
6. Rigden 5.
7. Qtd. in Brian 130.
8. Qtd. in Clark 204.
9. Qtd. in Clark 202.
10. Qtd. in Clark 175.
11. Qtd. in Rigden 9-10.
12. Kenji Sugimoto, *Albert Einstein: A Photographic Biography*, trans. Barbara Harshav (New York: Schocken Books, 1989) 57.
13. Brian 356.
14. Brian 380.
15. Brian 210-211.

Chapter 4

1. Pais, *"Subtle Is the Lord"* 525.
2. Qtd. in Clark 232.
3. Qtd. in Clark 237.
4. Qtd. in Clark 238.
5. Qtd in Brian 235.
6. Qtd. in Clark 247.
7. Qtd. in Clark 249.
8. Albert Einstein and Leopold Infeld, *The Evolution of Physics* (Cambridge, 1938), 251-252, qtd. in Clark.

9. Qtd. in Rigden 141.

10. Qtd. in Clark 220.

11. Qtd. in Brian 148.

12. Qtd. in Clark 70.

13. Otto R. Frisch, *What Little I Remember* (New York: Cambridge University Press, 1979) 22.

14. Pais, *Niels Bohr's Times, in Physics, Philosophy, and Polity* (Oxford: Clarendon Press, 1991), 154.

15. Pais, *Niels Bohr's Times* 179.

16. Qtd. in Rigden 142-143.

17. Qtd. in Rigden 100.

18. *The Official Web Site of the Nobel Foundation*, <http://www/nobel.se/physics/laureates/1921/index.html>

19. *The Official Web Site of the Nobel Foundation*, <http://www/nobel.se/physics/laureates/1922/index.html>

20. Clark 319.

21. "Presentation Speech by Professor A. A. Arrhenius, Chairman of the Nobel Committee for Physics of the Royal Swedish Academy of Sciences," *The Official Web Site of the Nobel Foundation*, <http://www/nobel.se/physics/laureates/1922/press.html>

22. Qtd. in Bernstein 194.

23. Clark 340.

24. Clark 340.

25. Clark 341.

26. Max Born, "Physics and Metaphysics," *The Scientific Monthly,* May 1956: 234.

27. Werner Heisenberg, "Reminiscences from 1926 and 1927," *Niels Bohr: A Centenary Volume,* ed. A. P. French and P. J. Kennedy (Cambridge, MA: Harvard University Press, 1985) 171.

28. Brian 164.

29. Bernstein 220.

30. Brian 305.

31. Brian 330.

32. Brian 339.

Chapter 5

1. Qtd. in Clark 181.

2. Qtd. in Rigden 14.

3. Qtd. in Clark 219.

4. Qtd. in Pais, *Einstein Lived Here* 171.

5. Qtd. in Pais, *Einstein Lived Here* 172.

6. Bernstein 213.

7. Clark 257-258.

8. Brian 113.

9. Clark 262.

10. Thomas Powers, *Heisenberg's War: The Secret History of the German Bomb* (New York: Alfred A. Knopf, 1993) 36.

11. Bernstein 211.

12. Clark 293.

13. Brian 188.

14. Stephen Hawking, "A Brief History of Relativity," *Time Magazine,* 27 Dec. 1999 <http://www-mat.upc.es/~comellas/GR.html>

15. Brian 219.

16. Brian 223.

17. Brian 226.

18. Brian 231.

19. Brian 237.

20. Clark 452.

21. Brian 237.

22. Brian 238.

23. Brian 350.

24. Brian 249.

Chapter 6

1. Qtd. in Pais, *Einstein Lived Here* 200.

2. Qtd. in Pais, *Einstein Lived Here* 25.

3. Qtd. in Brian 175.

4. Qtd. in Pais, *"Subtle Is the Lord"* 347.

5. Qtd. in Brian 350.

6. Qtd. in Brian 290.

7. Qtd. in Kai Bird and Martin J. Sherwin, *American Prometheus: The Triumph and Tragedy of J. Robert Oppenheimer* (New York: Alfred A. Knopf, 2005) 380.

8. Qtd. in Brian 331.

9. Qtd. in Brian 339.

10. Qtd. in Bernstein 221.

11. Qtd. in Brian 334.

12. Bernstein 214.

13. Naomi Pasachoff, *Niels Bohr, Physicist and Humanitarian* (Berkeley Heights, NJ: Enslow Publishers, Inc., 2003) 79-81.

14. Brian 310.

15. Brian 317.

16. Clark 556.

17. Qtd. in Brian 420.

18. "Letters reveal Einstein torn, defensive over atomic bombings of Japan," <http://www.physorg.com/news4928.html>

19. Qtd. in Brian 363.

20. Pais, *"Subtle Is the Lord"* 530.

21. Pais, *Einstein Lived Here* 241.

22. Pais, *Einstein Lived Here* 242.

23. Ed Regis, *Who Got Einstein's Office? Eccentricity and Genius at the Institute for Advanced Study* (Reading, MA: Addison-Wesley Publishing Company, Inc., 1987) 41.

Chapter 7

1. Bernstein 173-174.

2. Bernstein 171.

3. Bernstein 172.

4. Gale E. Christianson, *Isaac Newton and the Scientific Revolution* (New York: Oxford University Press, 1996) 94.

5. Christianson 83.

6. Clark 299.

7. Christianson 70.

8. Christianson 70-71.

9. Christianson 125.

10. J. Robert Oppenheimer, *Atom and Void: Essays on Science and Community* (Princeton, NJ: Princeton University Press, 1989) 10.

11. J. Robert Oppenheimer, *The Flying Trapeze: Three Crises for Physicists* (New York: Harper Clophon Books, 1964) 8.

12. Jaime Sayen, *Einstein in America* (Crown, New York: 1985) 289.

13. Brian 430.

14. Bird & Sherwin 380.

15. J. Robert Oppenheimer, "On Albert Einstein," in *Einstein: A Centenary Volume*, ed. A. P. French (Cambridge, MA: Harvard University Press, 1979) 48.

J. ROBERT OPPENHEIMER

1. Kai Bird and Martin J. Sherwin, *American Prometheus: The Triumph and Tragedy of J. Robert Oppenheimer* (New York: Alfred A. Knopf, 2005) 18.

2. Qtd. in Jeremy Bernstein, *Einstein* (New York: The Viking Press, 1973) 11.

3. David C. Cassidy, *J. Robert Oppenheimer and the American Century* (New York: Pi Press, 2005) 61.

4. Cassidy 63-64.

5. Qtd. in Bird & Sherwin 23, 42, 43.

6. Qtd. in Bernstein 40.

7. Qtd. in Bernstein 36.

8. Qtd. in Bernstein 53.

9. Qtd. in Bernstein 53.

10. Bernstein 32.

11. Bird & Sherwin 88.

12. Bernstein 48.

13. Qtd. in Bird & Sherwin 90.

14. Bernstein viii.

15. Qtd. in Bernstein 76.

16. Qtd. in Bernstein 79.

17. Qtd. in Jennet Conant, *109 East Palace: Robert Oppenheimer and the Secret City of Los Alamos* (New York: Simon & Schuster, 2005) 68.

18. Bernstein 82.

19. Bernstein viii.

20. Qtd. in Bernstein 97-98.

21. Qtd. in Bernstein 199.

22. Qtd. in Bernstein 89.

23. Qtd. in Bird & Sherwin 329.

24. Qtd. in Bernstein 119.

25. Qtd. in Bernstein 120.

26. Qtd. in Bird & Sherwin 443.

27. Qtd. in Bernstein 96.

28. Qtd. in Bernstein 152.

29. Qtd. in Bird & Sherwin 534.

30. Qtd. in Bernstein 159.

31. Qtd. in Bernstein 166.

32. Qtd. in J. Robert Oppenheimer Centennial at Berkeley. <http://ohst.berkeley.edu/oppenheimer/exhibit/chapter5.html>

Recommended Reading

BOOKS

Bernstein, Jeremy. *Oppenheimer.* Chicago: Ivan R. Dee, 2004.

Bird, Kai, and Sherwin, Martin J. *American Prometheus: The Triumph and Tragedy of J. Robert Oppenheimer.* New York: Knopf, 2005.

Brian, Denis. *Einstein.* New York: Wiley, 1996.

Calaprice, Alice. *The Einstein Almanac.* Baltimore: Johns Hopkins, 2005.

Cassidy, David C. *J. Robert Oppenheimer and the American Century.* New York: PI, 2005.

Clark, Ronald W. *Einstein: The Life and Times.* New York: Avon, 1984.

Fara, Patricia. *Newton.* New York: Columbia Univ. Pr., 2002.

Feingold, Mordechai. *The Newtonian Moment: Isaac Newton and the Making of Modern Culture.* New York: Oxford, 2004.

Gleick, James. *Isaac Newton.* New York: Pantheon, 2003.

Gribbin, John R. and Mary. *Annus Mirabilis: 1905, Albert Einstein, and the Theory of Relativity.* New York: Chamberlain Bros., 2005.

Pais, Abraham. *"Subtle Is the Lord— "The Science and the Life of Albert Einstein.* New York: Oxford, 1982.

Rigden, John S. *Einstein 1905.* Cambridge: Harvard Univ. Pr., 2005.

Severance, John B. *Einstein.* New York: Clarion., 1999.

Wolfson, Richard. *Simply Einstein.* New York: Norton, 2003.

WEB SITES

Albert Einstein Archives Online. <http://www.albert-einstein.org>

"All Was Light: Isaac Newton's Revolutions," The Huntington Library, Art Collections, and Botanical Gardens. 5 March-12 June 2005.

<http://www.huntington.org/LibraryDiv/Newton/Newtonexhibit.htm>

"Einstein's Big Idea," *NOVA*, Public Broadcasting Service. <http://www.pbs.org/wgbh/nova/einstein/>

"The Nobel Prize in Physics 1921." Official website of the Nobel Foundation. <http://nobelprize.org/physics/laureates/1921/einstein-bio.html>

"Oppenheimer: A Life," U. of California, Berkeley. <http://ohst.berkeley.edu/oppenheimer/exhibit/>

Glossary

alchemy *(AL kuh me)* a blend of pseudoscience, magic, and mystical philosophy in which people tried to change less costly metals into silver and gold.

amplitude the vertical distance from the crest of an electromagnetic wave to the level of the wave at rest.

atomic bomb a bomb that releases huge amounts of energy through the splitting of the *nuclei* (cores) of plutonium or uranium atoms.

big bang a theory that a cosmic explosion gave birth to the universe.

black hole a region of space in which the gravitational force is so strong that nothing can escape from it.

comet an icy body that normally travels around the sun in a long, oval orbit.

electromagnetic waves related patterns of electric and magnetic force that are generated by the *oscillation* (movement back and forth) of electric charges.

general theory of relativity the theory of Albert Einstein that explains the force of gravitation.

gravitational lens a massive object—typically a galaxy—lying along our line of sight to a more distant object; the mass of the gravitational lens bends the light of the distant object, splitting it into two or more images as seen from Earth.

ionize *(Y uh nyz)* the production of electrically charged atoms when high-energy particles or rays penetrate matter.

kinetic energy the energy of movement.

neutron *(NOO tron)* a subatomic particle with no electrical charge.

neutron star the smallest and densest type of star known, formed when a large star runs out of fuel.

nuclear fission the splitting of the nucleus of an atom into two nearly equal parts.

nuclear fusion the joining of the nuclei of two atoms to form the nucleus of a heavier element.

nucleus the tiny region at the center of an atom.

particle accelerator a device that speeds up the movement of *ions* (electrically charged atoms) or electrically charged subatomic particles to discover and study the particles and the forces that govern them.

photon *(FOH tahn)* the elementary particle that makes up light and all other forms of electromagnetic radiation.

proton *(PROH tahn)* a positively charged subatomic particle.

refraction the change (bend) in the direction in which waves travel when they pass from one kind of matter into another.

spectroscope *(SPEHK truh skohp)* an instrument that spreads out light into a spectrum by using a telescope.

spectrum the band of colors formed when a beam of white light is broken up by passing through a prism or by other means.

supernova an exploding star that can become billions of times as bright as the sun before gradually fading from view.

string theory a theory proposing that incredibly tiny loops of energy form the most basic stuff of everything in the universe, including all matter and all forces.

quanta *(KWON tuh)* the packets of energy that light consists of.

quantum mechanics the field of physics that describes the structure of the atom and the motion of atomic particles, as well as how atoms absorb and give off energy as light.

Index

Page numbers in *italic* type refer to pictures.